# The Disabled Body in
# Contemporary Art

# The Disabled Body in Contemporary Art

Ann Millett-Gallant

palgrave
macmillan

The Disabled Body in Contemporary Art
Copyright © Ann Millett-Gallant, 2010.
All rights reserved.

First published in 2010 by PALGRAVE MACMILLAN® in the United States –
a division of St. Martin's Press LLC, 175 Fifth Avenue, New York, NY 10010.

Where this book is distributed in the UK, Europe and the rest of the world,
this is by Palgrave Macmillan, a division of Macmillan Publishers Limited,
registered in England, company number 785998, of Houndmills, Basingstoke,
Hampshire RG21 6XS.

Palgrave Macmillan is the global academic imprint of the above companies
and has companies and representatives throughout the world.

Palgrave® and Macmillan® are registered trademarks in the United States, the
United Kingdom, Europe and other countries.

ISBN: 978-0-230-10406-8

Library of Congress Cataloging-in-Publication Data

Millett-Gallant, Ann, 1975–

   The disabled body in contemporary art / Ann Millett-Gallant.
      p. cm.
   Includes bibliographical references.
   ISBN 978-0-230-10406-8 (alk. paper)
   1. People with disabilities in art. 2. Art, Modern—20th century—Themes,
motives. 3. Art, Modern—21st century—Themes, motives. 4. Art and
society—History—20th century. 5. Art and society—History—21st century.
I. Title.

   N8236.P4M55 2010
   704.9'42—dc22

                  2009050872

A catalogue record of the book is available from the British Library.

Design by MPS Limited, A Macmillan Company

First edition: August 2010

10 9 8 7 6 5 4 3 2 1

Printed in the United States of America.

Transferred to Digital Printing in 2011

# Contents

# List of Figures

# Acknowledgments

Many talented individuals contributed to the pages of this book. I would like to thank fellow disability studies scholars, Alex Lubet, Rosemarie Garland-Thompson, Petra Kuppers, Ann Fox, Katie Lebesco, Simi and David Linton, Tobin Siebers, Brenda Breuggemann, Bruce Henderson, Mark Sherry, and Michael M. Chemers, for their editorial support and encouragement. Many artists and art historians likewise contributed ideas and constructive criticism, including Carol Mavor, Mary Sheriff, Kevin Parker, Jill Casid, elin o'Hara slavick, and Susan Harbage Page. I would like to thank photographer Joel-Peter Witkin for his inspiration and assistance. In addition to Page and Witkin, I must thank the artists whose work inspires me and illustrates this book: Sandie Yi, Marc Quinn, Ricardo Gil, and Riva Lehrer. The members of my writing group, with whom I shared many drafts and cups of coffee, deserve recognition as both colleagues and old friends: Elizabeth Howie, Leisa Rundquist, Betsy Towns, Pam Whedon, Lindsay Twa, and Laurel Frederickson. Finally, I would like to acknowledge my family, most especially my stepsister and accomplice, Brandee Gruener, my father and coach, Steve Millett, my mother and biggest fan, Pat Millett, and my husband, the Renaissance man, Paul Gallant.

Introduction

# Enabling the Image

In *Remembrance of an Open Wound* (1938), Mexican artist Frida Kahlo painted herself seated in a chair against a barren landscape, staring with an unyielding and unashamed returned gaze at the viewer and lifting her Tehuana-Mexican dress to display her bare legs. Her left leg, which caused the artist pain and impairments throughout her life due to childhood polio and an accident on a Mexico City bus at the age of eighteen, is wounded by leafy thorns and spurts blood onto her dress. Her left foot, which was amputated at the end of her life in the 1950s, is pictured bandaged and also bleeding. Roots that sprout from Kahlo's body and connect it to nature, a crown of flowers and thorns on her head, and the thorny site of her seemingly self-inflicted scars evoke imagery of Aztec sacrifice and healing rituals, as well as Christian martyrdom, influences characteristic of Kahlo's oeuvres. The title of the painting appears on a flowing ribbon within the composition, reminiscent of Mexican *retablos*, devotional images of creolized Mexican-Indian/Catholic saints performing healing rituals that were painted on wood panels and were quite popular in modern Mexican religious and vernacular culture. Themes of self-scarring and martyrdom in this work have been related to Kahlo's biography and disabilities, the many infidelities of her husband (Mexican muralist and painter Diego Rivera), and specifically a recent sexual affair between Rivera with Kahlo's sister, Cristina Kahlo.[1] Lifting the elaborate native Indian dress she was known for wearing, in this painting Kahlo reveals her wounds, and yet, a strictly biographical reading of these wounds veils their potent symbolism within the multireferential composition.

Surpassing reference to one specific event, Kahlo's wounds are psychic, sexual, and corporeal, as her wounded and painted body is marked by her personal and cultural history. The dress itself represents intersections between cultural signs and Kahlo's individual style and has been a detail misunderstood, in my opinion, by many viewers who make assumptions about her body as broken, wounded, and degenerate due to her disabilities. Kahlo's main biographer, Hayden Herrera, and many others have suggested that Kahlo wore such dresses to "hide" her limp and the scars from her accident and many surgeries, ignoring the period trend among the intellectual elite to wear such costume as a symbol of Mexican Nationalism. Further, as depicted in this painting, the dress serves as an instrument of revealing and concealing and Kahlo's mediation of her disabilities for the public. She raises her skirt to reveal the wounds, placed strategically and erotically on the upper thigh, yet she holds the hem down over the space at the center of the canvas to which the viewer's eyes are drawn—between her parted legs. In her painted self-image, Kahlo performatively covers and simultaneously flaunts her sex with manipulation of the dress. The dress frames and showcases the wounds she purposively displays for the viewer, as her brightly colored, elaborately patterned and ornamental costumes in real life would have attracted additional attention to her body. These dresses become a means for ornamentation and glorification of the body, and a means for the wearer, or performer, to self-direct the stares her body received in everyday life, due to her limp and other impairments.

*Remembrance of an Open Wound* is one of over a hundred self-portraits, many executed from Kahlo's bed during times of convalescence with an elaborately staged easel and overhead mirror. These self-portraits often display Kahlo's personal and medical body histories in images of her numerous miscarriages, surgeries, recoveries, and physical degeneration. The "self" portrayed in Kahlo's work emerges as a body in pieces—graphically ripped apart, wounded, bleeding, and impaled. Other works in her oeuvres document her friends, family, Native Indian, German, and Spanish-Mexican heritages, medical experiences, personal tragedies, daily domestic life in early twentieth-century Mexico, and her international travels. Each work is a carefully choreographed, symbolically and visually dense, not to mention colorful composition, rather than a one-dimensional depiction of her "suffering," a characteristic reading of Kahlo's paintings that has overshadowed their rich significances. Kahlo's paintings serve as public performances of identity whose significances and legacy exceed the frames of her disabled body, as well as the frames of her historical context. Kahlo's work falls before the contemporary time period that is the focus of this book, but her influence looms large in contemporary artworks, as well as in my analyses of them. Kahlo was ahead of her time in her unashamed, graphic, and performative bodily displays of disability. Many more recent artists have drawn inspiration and vivid imagery from Kahlo's compositions, for a range of reasons. California-based artist Carmen Lomas Garza was instrumental in reintroducing Kahlo's work to the public in the 1970s, particularly to a next generation of Hispanic artists and audiences. Lomas Garza's many prints of her Chicano/a home life and neighborhoods feature cultural and everyday heroes of the barrio, some without their lower left limbs and some using wheelchairs, actively engaged in social activities, such as in the depiction of a neighborhood social game in *Loteria-Table Llena*, (1972). Lomas Garza's images display acts of disabled people as everyday occurrences in community life. Her curatorial work with Kahlo's paintings has introduced her own ongoing influence by Kahlo and has helped Kahlo to become an artistic hero in the Chicano/a arts and rights movements of the 1970s and beyond, as contemporary artists include images of Kahlo and her naïve Mayan and Aztec imagery in their political work. Kahlo's inclusion of creolized (Mexican-Indian/Catholic) religious themes has also inspired the work of Kathy Vargas, which includes many traditional Mexican and Mexican-American objects of heal-ing and other miracles (*milagros,* often in the form of body parts, flowers, and other ritual objects believed to be incarnated by spirits), derived from ancient Mayan and Aztec spirituality. Kahlo's imagery of her body in pieces and ancient rituals (such as sacrifice) translates to photographs inspired by Vargas's work with AIDS and hospice patients, the deaths of her grandparents, and most profoundly, her mother's illness. In *Broken Column: Mother* (1997), Vargas creates a cross shape in separate collaged photographs, many based on spinal X-rays, of an ailing, prostrate body that directly references Kahlo's *The Broken Column* (1944), Kahlo's self-portrait with her spine in pieces and her torso surrounded by a medical brace. Vargas's works become ritual objects in their own rights, as Kahlo's imagery functions in the transformative powers of healing.

Kahlo's work also captured the attention of the predominantly white feminist art movement. In the 1970s, many feminist artists and scholars explored the politics of gender in the art world, worked to resurrect underrecognized female artists of the past, and revived traditional female arts and crafts practices, disrupting traditional and gendered hierarchies of art practices. In this spirit, Miriam Schapiro began making quilts and other collage works inspired by and including images of female artists whose work had been previously excluded from or trivialized by the canon of art history. These works evolved over time and expanded to series, such as *Collaboration Series: Frida Kahlo and Me* (c. 1988–1993). This series of mixed-media collages (including, for examples, *Time*, *Conservatory*, and *Agony in the Garden*, which is also based on *The Broken Column*) were modeled after prominent works by Kahlo and became a means for Schapiro to collaborate with Kahlo on new works and to identify with her as a female artist. Using paint, fabric, paper, and glitter, Schapiro glorifies Kahlo's self-portraits, many of which display Kahlo's body in pieces and in pain, and Kahlo's personal history in contemporary feminist works.

Anne Finger's fictional essay, "Helen and Frida," (1997) draws the legend and images of Kahlo into a self-portrait fantasy story and narrative of disability activism. The tale opens with Finger as a young girl, recovering from surgery with her leg in a plaster cast, watching old Hollywood movies, and being swept away by her own couch potato reverie. The narrator imagines herself on a film set shooting a campy plot between Helen Keller and Frida Kahlo, the latter of whom Finger plays the role in her fantasy. This imagined performance contradicts conventional narratives of pity, deficiency, and isolation that characteristically surround disabled women. The short story and the dream described within it reclaim and reframe the passionate lives and exploited bodies of these famous "disabled" women; Finger writes:

> So now the two female icons of disability have met: Helen, who is nothing but, who swells to fill up the category, sweet Helen with her drooping dresses covering drooping bosom, who is Blind and Deaf, her vocation; and Frida, who lifts her skirt, to reveal the gaping, cunt-like wound on her leg, who rips her body open to reveal her

back, a broken column, her back corset with its white canvas straps framing her beautiful breasts, her body stuck with nails; but she can't be Disabled, she's Sexual."[2]

Finger describes how Keller has problematically become a one-dimensional representation of a "Disabled" body, with no other identity or subjectivity, and how Kahlo' excessive persona and biographical legends have eclipsed her disability in popular imagination. The dress again serves as a central image for comparison and an object for interpretive and performative manipulation, while Finger also points to two familiar, explicit paintings of Kahlo's body. In addition, Finger rewrites the portrayal of these and other disabled women in Hollywood films and various forms of visual culture as suffering, asexual, and seeking cure, most often through the so-called benevolent and selfless help of a doctor or lover. She portrays both women as passionate and sensual, rather than corporeally and sensorially "lacking" and helplessly dependent. Homoerotic interactions between the women bring the story to a climax. The narrative—Finger's dream—of these two women spans and transgresses multiple moments and junctures in Finger's life, history, and memory; further, the story documents Finger's self-awareness and coming out as a disabled woman.

As a sampling of artists deeply affected by Kahlo's legacy, Lomas Garza, Schapiro, Vargas, and Finger produce works in mixed media that perform their mixed social and cultural identities. All have been drawn to and identified with Kahlo for their own for specific reasons, because of interests in gender, race, sexuality, and disability. All are drawn to Kahlo's defiant assertion of her body and its many stages, images, and transfigurations and her adamant exhibition of this body as the site of and source for artistic production and personal expression. All these themes emerge in particular forms in Kahlo's and these later artists' works, yet none of them are exclusive. Uniting the works are themes of the struggle to make artwork about the body in a sexist, racist, homophobic, and ableist world—a world from which a body such as Kahlo's has been largely rejected and analytically misunderstood.

Merging the fields of art history and disability studies, the following chapters explore what one can learn about art from the perspective of disability (as exemplified by my viewing of Kahlo's dress) and, in exchange, what one can learn about disability through contemporary art. This period in art (late 1960s to present) sets the stage for relevant themes of self-exhibition, identity, and the role of the body in art and society, as well as introduces significant use of photography and performance art as mediums for bodily representation. Disability studies as a discipline likewise appears on the scene during this period, embodying and critically analyzing historical representations of disability. I underscore the necessity of and provide frameworks for placing works by disabled and nondis-abled artists in dialogues with one another and with larger visual histories, including visual art in all media, photography, popular media, film, performance, medical imagery, and the nineteenth- and early-twentieth-century freak show. I explain how these diverse visual histories all contribute to visualizing disability in material culture and society and particularly to the staging the disabled and disfigured body as a spectacle. Positioning contemporary artworks into these contexts frames them as deeply historical and multidimensional representations of disability. My key examples subvert the conventions of art, as well as conventions or norms for bodies in social life. Departing from conventional art historical readings, my analyses of these images grant agency to the performative subjects on display. I question the perceptions viewers may bring to displays of disability in art and in everyday life, and my interpretative analyses enable the viewer to challenge stereotypical assumptions and to experience art and art history from disability studies perspectives. Such methods have yet to permeate art history to the extent that they inform fields of literature, film, theater, and performance. This book begins to mend these art historical oversights.

## Disability Studies and the Body

Disability studies has emerged in the last quarter of the twentieth century as a discipline that unites political activism, sociology, critical cultural analyses, and creative production. Particularly since the 1990s, the humanities have come forth in this field of scholarship, joining forces with the social and biological sciences in studying disability.[3] Exploring the experiences, subjectivity, representational frameworks for, and social and political barriers faced by disabled people, disability studies is a cultural studies of the body. Disability studies exhibits how the body may serve as a site, target, and vehicle for ideology and creative expression. Working to overturn predominant stereotypes about bodies and norms for social acceptability, disability studies may be used as a framework to deconstruct dominant practices of categorizing, portraying, and interpreting the representation of bodies in visual culture and in everyday life.

The field of disability studies is as varied as the many forms and experiences of "disability" itself, yet primary agendas emerge across much of the scholarship, such as problematizing medical models for disability. The culturally ubiquitous medical model views disability as a set of medical and corporeal "problems" and works to cure, fix, or eliminate these "problems" and consequently, disabled people, from the population.[4] In contrast, disability studies strives to establish a social model for disabled people as an oppressed group and forges alliances with theories and positions of other socially marginalized groups. The disability studies term "ableism" draws parallels to sexism, racism, classism, and homophobism to encompass multidimensional practices (networks of social policies, attitudes, and daily social exchanges) that marginalize disabled people. Whereas the medical model locates disability on and in the body as "abnormality" and privileges normalization or standardization of all bodies, a social model asserts that disability is constructed through environmental, social, and political apparatuses that work to exclude disabled people. A medical model suggests that the body should change, and a social model counters that ideology, policy, and attitudes need to change to accommodate, service, and provide equality for disabled people. Finally, the social model differentiates disability, as a socially constructed identity, from impairment, which refers to specific bodily configuration and its individual consequences for a subject's health, mobility, limitations, and other related experiences.

My attraction to disability studies is personal and professional, as are the connections I see between disability studies and art. I was born with congenital amputation and various so-called deformities of the limbs and mouth, a bodily configuration defined by some long, technical, Greek-derived medical term I will spare my readers, as I have spared myself from memorizing. My diagnosis states that my body was a result of an "intrauterine insult"; according to "objective" medical language for disability, something insulted my mother's uterus in the formation my body. My prognosis predicted no internal "problems," no chronic pain, a long life span, and high probability for adaption. The medical literature prescribes my syndrome's characteristic deformities as producing a "birdlike" appearance; these facial impairments were nothing that many frustrating years of semitorturous orthodontic experiments and hours of expensive, painful surgery (including some procedures that never worked) couldn't "fix," for the most part. Although I appear almost "normal" now in the face (and am often told that I'm attractive), and can speak well, my diagnosis didn't account for these forms of pain and strain. As for the rest of my body, I wear prosthetic legs and use a scooter or crutches for public mobility; at home, I maneuver more freely on the floor and use elevating stools. My range of activities and capabilities is wide. I've always known I was disabled, but for the most part, perhaps due to my adaptable motor, occupational, not to mention social skills, I have functioned quite well, and almost exclusively, in a nondisabled world. Medical technology, adequate financial resources, and family support have further enabled my independence and social acceptance.

I had not explored my identity as a disabled person and, for the most part, didn't talk about it, until I pursed my PhD in art history. My orthopedic therapy as a child included artistic projects, and in the arts at least, I never saw my disability as a hindrance, but rather an asset. In high school, a half-day vocational program became my personal quest to study anatomy, as I often painted fragmented and reaching bodies. I later majored in art history in college, while continuing my interests in figure drawing and painting. In a search for my academic niche in graduate school, I was mesmerized by disability studies and looking at disability in art. I found a special voice, one which addressed prevalent social and scholarly issues, but which also spoke to me. I've learned a lot about myself in my studies and in the process of producing this book. My reader will find pieces of me throughout—in some not so obvious places. I can only speak for my own experiences, as I have one specific form of impairment, not to mention one specific life in which it plays out. I do not justify the analyses that follow with my own disability, but rather, I here position my own subjective interpretations. Being disabled in society does lend me a perspective on some specific human experiences of marginalization, exclusion, and forms of oppression based on the body, as it also lends me a unique perspective for viewing art. Disability studies has helped me articulate these aspects of my own and my subjects' disabilities. I may see themes of disability operating in places others do not—in language, visual representation, and social attitudes.

My reader will hopefully benefit from these insights, even if to many I never seem "disabled"—at least according to initial impressions or mainstream definitions of the word. I'm visually physically different—"disabled" or "handicapped" in conventional language, so of course I must know about being disabled—I must be interested in disability, and yet, what does that mean, to be interested in disability? Despite that I wear my disability on my exterior like a flashing light everyday, and like a suit of armor on every social, personal, and professional stage I enter, disability has been a challenging subject for analyses. Mainstream culture teaches disabled people that our success is intrinsically tied to the denial of our disabilities and our bodies. If we are successful ("able"), we must "overcome" our disability—effectively defeat our impairments—and become as normal as possible, for, we are told, this is the goal. In the process, our debased, so-called degenerate bodies may become a source of resentment. Such dynamics operating in society have impacted the experiences of many, in forms such as mainstreaming into "normal" classes, because one is too smart for the "special" class, or hearing acceptance expressed through others declaring, "She's just like everybody else." It is perhaps only in adulthood I have begun to realize that striving to be "like everyone else" might not be such a worthwhile enterprise. In the first place, what exactly defines this "everybody else" from whom disabled people appear in contradistinction? Secondly, why, according to these sentiments, is human homogeneity socially preferable?

People with disabilities are intrinsically heterogeneous. Disability studies faces the challenge of defining "the disabled" as a group, because of the range of impairments and experiences encompassed. Further, disability as an identity marker differs according to an individual's race, gender, class, background, and sexual orientation. Disability may only be characterized by difference from and exclusion by the "norm" or dominant culture, and various, often random, experiences shared by individuals. Disability studies theorist Lennard J. Davis's (1995) historicizing of the concept of "normal" in Western culture and its emergence as a component of social oppression greatly informs this work.[5] Disability displays not just an opposition to, but also a resistance to conformity, standardization, and the "normal"; in this project, I fixate on artistic examples that revel in corporeal difference, deviance, and abnormal disfigurement, specifically through visual displays of the body. Perhaps more vividly than other markers of identity, disability and its "otherness," or deviation from the norm, is inscribed on the body and attracts attention to the body's visible and functional irregularities. Visibly disabled bodies are marked and attract sometimes unwanted attention.

Disabled people often become social spectacles. Perhaps, however, it is what one does with social attention that matters—perhaps the body on display (the spectacle) can utilize its voyeuristic attention through artistic and political acts. In this case, the body is far from "overcome," for, as I will argue, in strategic acts of self-exhibition, the disabled or disfigured body becomes the source of creative and intellectual productions, as exemplified by Kahlo's and many other artists' influential work. In addition, disability has been a motivation and critical perspective with which I have produced this book, one that then becomes a form of self-exhibition. However, this notion of disability as critical method is counterintuitive to predominant social stereotypes. Predominant beliefs purport disability as a limitation engendered in the body, not as an opportunity for alternative or unique perspectives. Scholars involved in disability studies (both disabled and nondisabled) and disability rights follow in the legacies of other civil rights and academic movements. Like other marginalized peoples, disabled people refuse to conform to, and fight against, unaccommodating and often demeaning standards and the cultural structures that uphold them.

Disability studies draws insight from other related minority scholarship on the political, social, and personal consequences of cultural representation particularly. Mainstream representation, through repeated conventions, produces images of disability, often in forms which not only fail to account for the breadth of impairments and related dimensions of human experiences, but which also create false and harmful models for disability, or perhaps worse, eclipse the bodily and social reality of disability altogether. Disabled people share and often embody and combat long histories of being exploited and portrayed derogatorily in visual culture, while being simultaneously shamed, stigmatized, and politically erased. Quite often, disabled characters in literature, film, television, art, and other media are symbols of something else, something tragic or derogatory, such as social decay or psychic breakdown, and display these symbolic connotations on their bodies. Thus, disability is largely associated with disaster, something to be avoided and feared, rather than as a multidimensional, intensely embodied reality. Even more tragically, these popular representations are often the only experiences some audiences have with disability, as visual culture constructs images of disability in society that affect public policy and result in discriminatory and hurtful daily social interactions.

The public ignorance about disability is furthered by the silence such environments enforce among disabled people. Like other forms of false racist, sexist, classist, and homophobic cultural images and subsequent stereotypes, these ableist representations may be internalized, often diminishing personal development and self-esteem and informing how disabled people see themselves and other disabled people. Compared with other critical theories of identity, disability studies, I believe, pushes further its explorations of the significance of the body in representation for subjectivity and political status. I draw predominantly from disability studies scholarship that critiques such representations in visual culture, yet I also complicate them to enable other, more varied perceptions.[6] Representations of the body make a difference for those with bodily difference from the norm. Body images—images we have of ourselves, largely informed by those produced by cultural representation— matter in art and everyday life.

### Visualizing Disability

The politics of artistic and social representation are strikingly substantial for and specific to people with disabilities. Being physically "different" is being unique, standing out (or sitting down) in a crowd, and receiving fervent and sometimes condescending attention—particularly in the form of the "stare," as best theorized by literary and disability studies theorist Rosemarie Garland-Thomson (1997).[7] Garland-Thomson conflates the theoretical gaze, often discussed in feminist and postcolonial critical analyses of representation as a mechanism of domination and violence, with the stare—a pervasive, tangible gaze that the disabled confront on a daily basis. This gaze/stare, for Garland-Thomson, distances the disabled body from the nondisabled viewer, constructing the disabled individual as an inferior and undesirable "other." The stare, based on the medical model of disability, attempts to diagnose the disabled "other" in order to confirm the nondisabled spectator's normality. In a later work, Garland-Thomson (2008) further historicizes and complicates the dynamics and dimensions of staring, adding more empowering examples to her repertoire.[8] Visually "marked" on the body, disabled people are spectacles on the stages of various cultural venues as well as everyday life. These bodies are on display because of their deviance from the norms.

Garland-Thomson (2001) also elaborates on these frameworks as they function in photography specifically. Because the camera has served as an instrument of science historically, and because the realist mode of photographs present the illusion of unmediated access to the bodies they display[9] (indeed both clinical and pornographic), Garland-Thomson argues that photography is engaged specifically in problematic dynamics of diagnostic gazing and staring at bodies.[10] She identifies the discourses of disability operating in photographs under four formal and interpretive rhetorics: the wondrous, the sentimental, the exotic, and the realistic, stressing that these rhetorics necessarily overlap in each image. In other words, representations cannot conform to categories of perception, and no representation is purely one-dimensional.[11] Poignantly, her examples (mainly images drawn from charity publications, fashion advertising, and "special interest" media stories) are contemporary and commercial translations of multiple historical discourses on disability. This method exhibits that, counter to linear narratives, one historical model for disability does not neatly expand upon or eclipse a previous one. Discourses on and representations of disability therefore recycle across visual and historical contexts. Significantly, Garland-Thomson argues that images produce social discourses on and contribute to the social construction of disability, due specifically to their photographic form and how it constructs disability as spectacle; in addition to producing "reality," photography provides a means for reproducing and circulating problematic images of disability, as well as provides the opportunity for the distanced viewer to stare at and diagnose the disabled body. Garland-Thomson's specific application of the gaze/stare to the analysis of photography evolves from photographer and disability studies theorist David Hevey's (1992) notion that photography "enfreaks" disabled people, thus socially and visually constructing them as freakish, ostracized "others."[12] Indeed, as I will argue, photography often voyeuristically offers up the body, particularly the disabled and disfigured body, on a platter. Garland-Thomson extends her theories to disabled performance artists, whom she argues solicit the stare to confront the spectator and effectively "talk back."[13]

Garland-Thomson's analysis of commercial photographs and the performances of disabled people inform my interpretation of contemporary art images. Yet these analyses are largely pessimistic about representations of disability and disfigurement, particularly those by nondisabled people. In order to mine more deeply these connections between staring and gazing, specifically in art history, I turn toward examples from contemporary art that feature visibly noticeable corporeal deviance from the norm. The forms of disabled bodies I showcase are mainly individuals with physical impairments, more so than sensorial and developmental or intellectual, although all people with impairments are subject to the gaze/stare to varying degrees. Because of this emphasis, my examples are far from comprehensive as a survey of disability in contemporary art. I highlight also bodies I describe as "disfigured," which I sometimes conflate with disabled bodies, yet by "disfigured" I again connote a range of striking visible differences from the norm—bodies that capture attention due to their asymmetry, sizes, shapes, "missing" or extra features and limbs, or other qualities that may cause subjects to become social spectacles and to experience stigma and marginalization. The notion of disfigurement destabilizes concepts of "normal" versus "abnormal" and nondisabled versus disabled bodies, for disfigurement, to even a larger degree than corporeal disability, exists on a continuum and may be determined subjectively. Notions of "normal" versus disabled/disfigured bodies prove relative to perspective and mutually contingent—one characterization takes form only in the face of the other, and the particular characteristics of both alter according to time, place, and point of view.

Further, rather than explaining repeatedly how the gaze/stare and the cultural images that orchestrate it deliver oppression upon bodies, I choose to imagine multiple forms of staring and to destabilize the power dynamics therein. After all, the gaze/stare is not always "normal"; as a physically disabled and disfigured woman who studies visual culture and observes social interactions, I repeatedly gaze/stare at others. We live in a visual society, in which we are all pervasively gazing/staring at each other and forming our notions of ourselves both in identifications with and against other bodies. The gaze/stare in the following chapters is conceived as mutually constitutive and multidirectional, and it provides a medium for interaction with potentials for progressive social change. The gaze/stare enacts a mutual and altering exchange between the viewer, the image producer, and the body on display, as well an opportunity for a revision of cultural images.

Issues of political and artistic visibility come to the fore in discussions of images of disability in art. Disability studies–minded scholars and artists search for means to represent the body outside of and in subversion to dominant conventions, body standards, and norms for interpretation, without succumbing to the dangers of exploitation. Because of the hypervisibility of disability in daily life and in dominant representations as "other" (as outlined above), disabled image-producers may opt to avoid mainstream venues for art and performance. Disability studies scholar and performance artist Petra Kuppers (2003) maintains that the disabled body in artistic and everyday performance is able to violate conventional codes of difference, but only in specific forms and contexts, which she characterizes as "off-stage" or distinct from mainstream venues.[14] She argues that performances of the disabled are the most transgressive at the margins, because the center, defined by conventional frames of bodily representation, is saturated with problematic and consuming metaphors for disability. In the margins and marginal venues and in acts of veiling and concealing, Kuppers states, the disabled performer may exercise opportunistic visibility and invisibility.

Kuppers' work on disabled performers and artists greatly informs my thinking, particularly as it relates to performance theorist Peggy Phelan's (1993) questioning of the consequences of representation, particularly of the body, for subjects on display.[15] Phelan underscores how being visible and represented in visual culture by no means indicates nor substitutes for social and political visibility. In a most lucid and memorable quote, Phelan explains: "If representational visibility equals power, then almost-naked young white women should be running Western culture."[16] Further, Phelan underscores how visual media inevitably fails to express the self and identity through representation of the body—representations are constructed *images* that necessarily engage illusion in the simultaneous presence and absence of the human subject portrayed. Images often depict the desires of those who produce them rather than offering self-directed visibility of the subject depicted in them. Phelan argues for the power of withholding one's body from the economy of visual representation and exploitation of the mainstream, like Kuppers' performative "off-stage" examples. Finally, Phelan maintains that performance is the art form that most fully understands the potentials of disappearance, or invisibility, and offers the most means for exchange between the viewer and the spectacle. Phelan includes photography in her performative examples, as the viewer interacts visually with a material body performing before the camera. For Phelan, photography and performance art best exploit and critique the dubious aspects of representation for political means. For my analysis, performance art and photography therefore elicit and subvert the gaze/stare.

Self-exhibition is a risky practice and yet, as I will argue, many disabled artists and artist models choose to parade their abnormalities and display their spectacular bodies to shake notions of normality to the core. They solicit and reverse the gaze/stare and optimize their statuses as spectacles. The "spectacle" in the language of theater refers to visual attributes and qualities that elicit wonder. Designating a body, image, or object as a spectacle connotes its staged display in the presence of a spectator. The spectacle also implies a cross-cultural performance, in its longstanding associations with exhibitions of art, medicine, and theater. Finally, making a spectacle of oneself, in colloquial language, involves a conscious, albeit irrational or impassioned display that defies social norms for bodily behaviors and appearances and depends on the presence of a scrutinizing social stare. In this context, spectacles are stigmatized, yet being "spectacular" is being sensational, dramatic, and visually awe-inspiring. Throughout these chapters, unashamed performers make spectacular spectacles of themselves. Their agency lies in the power of self-representation and strategic, performative (in)visibility. These performative acts are shocking, often playfully so, confrontational, and revisionist. These artists manipulate the visual realm to their maximum advantage.

## Disabling Frameworks

The following chapters further underscore the necessity of viewing artworks by nondisabled and disabled artists side by side. I provide a fresh framework for placing images of disability in conversations with one another and with longer visual histories of *all* bodies. Often in scholarship, such works fall into inadequate and restrictive interpretive categories. The works of nondisabled artists that feature disability are largely misunderstood as one-dimensionally sensational, or are heavily criticized for circulating stereotypes and enacting oppression against the images' disabled subjects. Many discussions of these images often focus on discursively paralleling nondisabled artists' works with problematic medical, charity, and freak show images of disability. These are valid contexts for analyzing much of the artworks, yet provide limiting frameworks. For me, considering images of disability, from any source, as obviously shocking or as clearly rehashing medical models and notions of pity impairs viewers from seeing differently and effectively disables the subjects portrayed.

Disabled artists' works are also approached from restrictive frameworks. Disabled artists are unfortunately often disregarded by the mainstream audience or assumed to express images of so-called suffering (like Kahlo) and the desire to be "normal." Their work may be seen as acts of overcoming their disabilities and therefore forms of therapy and rehabilitation. Incorporating artmaking into therapy is a valid practice, and I would advocate for *all* people the idea of art production as a teachable, occupational "life skill" (as suggested by rehabilitation and occupational therapy practices); however, suggesting that disabled people make art strictly for these purposes implies that they are continuously striving to be "healthy" (meaning nondisabled) and in constant states of rehabilitation, rather than expressing through art their identities, knowledge, histories, and so on. Conversely to this mainstream perspective, many disabled artists are embraced by the disability community, a welcoming and empowering environment, yet their work remains unseen by the larger public and art world. The disability community may also omit or overlook larger art historical contexts when championing this work, which effectively keeps these disabled artists in isolation. My analyses strive to dismantle the divisions between nondisabled and disabled artists and art histories.

Looking at visual images of disabled bodies with a critical eye is crucial. From a disability studies perspective, I see the importance of interrogating the derogatory and dehumanizing tropes of disability operating in visual culture and revealing their roots and effects, particularly when not apparent to the viewer. I see the importance of championing the Disability Arts and Culture movement, a form of disability pride, which encourages disabled artists to make work about and with their bodies as a means to express the dimensionality of disability as a lived experience. However, from an art historical perspective, I avoid framing the work of disabled artists as preferably progressive, more "authentic" representations of disability, particularly in opposition to the work of nondisabled artists. The experience and symbolic meanings of disability are socially constructed and mediated for and by nondisabled *and* disabled people. Further, I strongly resist categorizing images as "positive" and "negative," for images are intricately deceptive, internally contradictory, and always subject to revision and contortion through interpretive acts. Notions of "positive" images would have to ignore the realities of social prejudice, rejection, exclusionary environments, and limited accessibility, which disabled people combat on a daily basis. In addition to mobility and functionality issues, impairment can cause real physical and emotional pain. To exclude these dimensions of disability would produce a superficial "positive" representation that reduces individual variation and the dimensions of images. Such concepts also demand the question: positive of/for whom? Notions of derogatory versus progressive, or subversive, representation depend on the eyes of the beholder. The transgressive potentials of these artworks exist in the acts of their interpretation.

Trained to gaze beyond the surface of images, I also strongly resist pigeonholing the work of nondisabled artists who feature disability into a category of "negative" depictions. I wouldn't know how to sum up such a category, no more than I would know how to craft an ideally "positive" image. Both result in reinscribing stereotypes and even empowering one-dimensional readings of artworks. For examples, I find the excessively bodily and macabre photographic work, much of which features amputees and amputated body parts, of Joel-Peter Witkin (c. 1970 to present) and the so-called freak photographic portraits of Diane Arbus (c. 1960–1970) intriguing, challenging, provocative, sometimes disturbing, and at other times (often simultaneously) visually alluring and enchanting. My readings of their and others' work do not disregard the objectifying aspects of the images, but rather explore the multiple and conflicting implications, adding shades of gray to the so-called blacks and whites. I see shadowed bodies that long to display their glory from behind the two dimensions of the photographic image. I place such images in dialogues, sometimes arguments with those of disabled artists; my mediation attempts to enable all images to agree to disagree. I prefer to ask *how* historical representation of disability is often disturbing, through examining viewer dynamics, rather than pointing out why. I am fascinated by how and why disability, or physical difference from the norm, is a transhistorical spectacle throughout visual culture. Why do we look, gaze, and stare at disabled bodies? I am continuously drawn to and confused by the dynamics of desire and repulsion and romanticization and fear that emerge from the historical viewing of disabled bodies on display.

Admittedly, much of this subject matter is quite challenging, and many of the images would be hard to rescue or completely harness for the empowerment of disabled people, if those were my goals. But perhaps there is something more productive to do with this so-called tainted visual history (in art, popular culture, medicine, and the freak show, for examples), which is far from bankrupt, as it continues to recycle and operate in contemporary culture and images. I believe that the "problem" exists not necessarily in the images, similarly to how the social model maintains that the "problem" is not inherent in the disabled body that needs "fixing" or "curing," but rather that what needs to change are the problematic, limiting social constructions and perceptions of disability in culture. What must change for progress to happen, and for our visual history to be a part of such a movement, are often our acts of viewing and interpreting. I indeed find troubling many of the assumptions and stereotypes about disability that come center stage when I survey the predominant scholarship on many nondisabled artists' work. I find such interpretive dialogues on these works often more objectifying of disability than the images themselves. I prefer to find disjuncture and slippage in signification and both potentially degrading *and* liberating aspects of the works. I desire to see more dimensions, more layers of meaning, in contemporary representations of disability.

My argument is interpretive, as I intervene on visual histories by adding to them alternative narratives of and perspectives on disability. My methods of comparative visual analyses aim to create a level playing field for nondisabled and disabled artists and their artworks. I unpack portrayals of disability in contemporary visual culture through comparisons with examples drawn from long and broad histories of bodily representation.

## The Acts

The following chapters center on contemporary artworks that feature visibly disabled bodies and draw these images into longer visual traditions. Within these pages, readers will meet legendary goddesses and mythical creatures; monsters, freaks, and human curiosities; corporeal objects of wonder; and more contemporary subjects of multimedia art, performance, and film. These bodies share histories of embodied performance and corporeal display, and therefore provide a legacy for contemporary art. Rather than attempting an exhaustive survey of disability in art (a task which would undoubtedly prove exhausting), I focus on particularly rich examples because of the histories they recall; these contemporary works draw predominantly from, and translate into contemporary terms, artistic traditions for representing the human form. Much of the works respond directly to art historical, figurative traditions, such as Classical and Neoclassical sculpture, portraiture, the conventional and nonconventional nude, social realist photography, and performance and body art. Simultaneously, they incorporate representations of the body, specifically the visibly disabled and disfigured body, found in medical displays, the freak show, and popular culture. I trace these histories of bodily display as they operate in contemporary art to force dialogues between contemporary artworks and historical images and contexts. This process, I argue, raises necessary questions about the prejudices and reservations viewers may bring to visions of the body, and disability, on display. My interpretations enable viewers to challenge these assumptions, to see art differently, and to uncover multiple dimensions to representations of disability.

Contemporary art provides fertile ground for these analyses. The art of this time period (c. 1960s to present) is contemporaneous with a number of civil rights movements, theoretical and artistic explorations of identity, interest in the dynamics of viewer reception, and an image explosion in our global, information-saturated culture. Further, much artwork of this period intentionally crosses traditional boundaries between artistic media, between art and life, and between art and other forms of visual culture—the merging of the "high" and the "low" arts. Contemporary art may be characterized by its irresolvable and contrary nature, as the works welcome and manipulate multiple interpretations. Such contemporary art therefore serves as an ideal medium for my disability studies–minded investigations of representation, for contemporary art is already fragmented, contingent, and ripe for interpretive interventions on traditional readings.

As described by art theorist Henry Sayre (1989), contemporary art, particularly performance and photography, refuses to be contained to any single context, viewer perception, or conventional attribution of meaning. Sayre uses the phrase "exceeds the frame" to describe such works' projection of meanings that reach beyond the image itself—beyond language, facts, and narrative—and enter into viewer's subjective, interpretive space.[17] The frame signifies both the physical edges of the art object, as well as the metaphorical divisions between the image, its social and historical context, and the viewer. Photography and performance artworks particularly, graphically exceed frames between the symbolism, corporeal materiality, mediation, and lived experiences of the body on display. Further, these media transgress frames, or contexts, of visual culture—entering into the realms of popular media, theater, and the performances of everyday life. In these images, my arguments surrounding the gravity of bodily representation for disabled social subjects bear the most weight. I also engage this phrase "exceeding the frame" throughout the following chapters to characterize artworks as dynamic and to describe interactive exchanges between spectators and spectacles and between images and social realities. My chosen examples respond to their rapidly changing, dynamic social contexts and take part in those changes.

Chapter 1, "Disarming Venus," opens with and focuses on a 1995 disarming performance piece by the Irish artist Mary Duffy, who was born without arms. Duffy's body on display recalls the canonical Venus de Milo visually, and she imparts an impassioned speech about her experiences of being shamed, objectified, and physically rejected by the medical profession and society at large. The piece confuses viewers' perceptions of the body as "whole" or "broken" in art and society. My analysis traces the tradition of the nude Venus as a trope that aestheticizes and objectifies the female body throughout art history. I place Duffy's performance in comparison with conventional and nonconventional Venus images, as the Venus tradition proves to both idealize and disfigure women's bodies. This tradition of the nude and its formal conventions are challenged specifically in feminist performance and body art from the 1970s onward, which serves as a legacy for Duffy's and other disabled and disfigured artists' self-representational work. I argue how disability studies perspectives, as elicited through Duffy's performance, provoke a revision of the Venus figure in art history. This chapter sets up a critical framework that weds disability studies with feminist body criticism, particularly surrounding theories of the gaze/stare, and introduces a performative framework for viewing images of the body in all art media throughout the following chapters.

Chapter 2, "Sculpting Body Ideals," centers on artist Marc Quinn's *Alison Lapper Pregnant* (2005). This monumental marble statue on display in London's Trafalgar Square is a nude, full body portrait of British resident and artist, Alison Lapper, who also was born without arms and with shortened legs. Featuring Lapper unclothed and seven months pregnant, the work makes a bold statement about the display of disability in the public realm. This work and the controversy surrounding it showcase disability issues at the fore of current debates in contemporary art. The work and Quinn's many previous marble sculptures of amputee models, in the series *The Complete Marbles* (2002), adopt the highly idealizing traditions and conventions of Neoclassicism, an art form characteristically employed for public statues to idealize political figures and the often patriarchal, moralistic, and nationalistic social values the figures personify. I argue how *Alison Lapper Pregnant* disrupts artistic and social ideals for bodies, therefore becoming an antimonument, and it simultaneously continues in traditions that purport public heroes. The work embodies the stereotypes of disability as heroic, tragic, *and* freakish and functions to make such stereotypes visible, part of public discourse, and open for debate. I underscore how artistic and historical contexts are crucial to interpreting the representation of the disabled body in art and public life. Lapper's own voice is a key component to these discussions of disability and artistic versus social representations, as are her self-portrait sculptures, photographs, and collages. By comparing Quinn's statue to Lapper's artwork, I illustrate the informative and beneficial results of viewing the work of nondisabled and disabled artists in dialogues.

The contemporary photography of Joel-Peter Witkin takes center stage in Chapter 3, "Performing Amputation." Many of his photographs feature disfigured models in excessive and theatrical displays. The compositions recall, parody, and strategically corrupt traditions of bodily representation found in Classical and Neoclassical sculpture, ornamental motifs, the art historical still life, medical exhibits and photographs, and the early modern freak show. With the amputee body and amputating techniques, Witkin dismembers and sutures together multiple visual traditions. Witkin takes on the history of art and photography and effectively performs amputation on their visual conventions as he performs literal surgery on his images. His personal touch on the photographic plate and print perverts the assumed neutrality of the photographic gaze. The camera has been used as an instrument of medicine and of the gaze historically, a history in which Witkin's images intervene. I argue that Witkin's controversial and excessive photographs disrupt medical models for disability by presenting disabled and disfigured bodies as objects of art, design, and aesthetic magnificence, particularly because of their curious and spectacular, abnormal bodies. His camera both references and enacts images of objectification by often displaying the body as an object. However, Witkin's amputee and other disfigured subjects elect and even request to be photographed; they therefore collaborate with Witkin in their production as photographic spectacles. As stages on which these models perform, the photographs may serve as venues for progressive self-exhibition and unashamed parading of the so-called abnormal body.

Chapter 4, "Exceeding the Frame," spotlights the photography of Diane Arbus, infamous for capturing the subcultural and abnormal "others" who populated her contemporary society, as well as her imagination. In this chapter, I unravel further my metaphor of exceeding frames, because Arbus's images reference multiple traditions of portraiture in the contexts of painting; art, commercial, documentary, clinical, and family album photography; and the live performances and photographs generated from the freak show. I center on Arbus's images of disabled and disfigured bodies, among her most famous "freak" photographs. I draw visual and discursive comparisons between Arbus's photographs and images drawn from various visual media, produced by disabled and nondisabled artists, which feature corresponding body types. Arbus's portraits of a giant, dwarfs, and a wheelchair-user in particular reveal how certain socially conspicuous individuals indeed combat a history of being portrayed as medical specimens, freakish others, and creatures of myth, particular to their embodiments. By exceeding the frames between the image and everyday life, Arbus's photographs challenge viewers' assumptions about certain bodies on display in art and society. Through analyzing the dubious and often contradictory discourses on bodily difference that operate within and beyond Arbus's photographic frames, I argue that the designations "normal" versus abnormal or "freak" depend on context and are interchangeable, particularly through the reversibility of the gaze.

My conclusion, "Staring Back and Forth," summarizes key points of previous chapters through personal narrative. I recount my experience of serving as a model for a Joel-Peter Witkin photograph, an event that I pursued. This story demonstrates major themes in this book, by allowing the object of representation to speak and perform and by elaborating on the experiences of disabled people.

# Disarming Venus

Disarming: - alluring, bewitching, and shocking
            - crippling, disabling, deactivating, and subjugating
            - removing arms and defenses

Irish artist Mary Duffy, born without arms, laid herself bare in a 1995 live performance.[1] The performance produced multiple acts of exposure: personal, political, and corporeal. Posing in the nude, Duffy revealed verbally how her disabled body is defined by medicine and society as lacking, inadequate, and undesirable. She reflected upon her confrontations with medical and social gazes and described how they impacted her own sense of self. Duffy's performative act transgressed the boundaries between representation and everyday life, as it simultaneously refigured histories of art and performance. Duffy's body as the armless nude invoked the Classical Venus de Milo, while at the same time offered itself as a vulnerable human being and naked, medicalized specimen. The performance showcased disability as the source and site of creative production and the disabled body as a work of art, while Duffy projected an empowered, self-mediated body image into the social arena. In a self-objectifying act, Duffy explained how her body was already objectified in society, and in the act of talking back, Duffy's monologue became social dialogue.

When the lights came up on stage, the viewer saw only Duffy's disarming naked form. Her unclothed, armless body remained motionless, like a statue, medical model, or frozen subject of a clinical photograph, as she spoke calmly and provocatively: "You have words to describe me," Duffy began in her condemnation of the medical profession: "Congenital malformation." Duffy remembered herself as a frightened child, searching for self-definition in the dictionary. "Congenital meant 'from birth,'" she stated, leaving the idea of "malformation" to the audience's imagination. She then addressed members of the public at large, who make her a spectacle through their stares, as she repeated the questions she has routinely received: "Were you born like that or did your mother take those dreadful tablets? Did you have an accident?" These intrusive questions are common in the social interactions of disabled people and are based on the assumption that because the visibly disabled body deviates from the norm, it is open for public scrutiny and diagnosis. These experiences represent acts of social stigma against and the shaming of disabled people. The negative reactions to her body,[2] according to Duffy, have included encouraging her to hide, deny her body, and remain invisible.

Duffy transformed conventional language, expressing how it feels to be "disabled"—spoken for, objectified, and disarmed, stating: "The doctors' words didn't fit me properly." She discredited these impersonal, offensive terms because they contradicted her own subjective experience: "I felt my body was right for me. . . . Whole, complete, functional." Duffy calmly expressed her anger at others' attempts to make her "whole," because such attitudes disregarded her own self-defined body image and feeling of completeness. In these experiences, Duffy confronted the pervasive medical model for disability, which suggests that disability is a medical problem to be rehabilitated or eliminated from the population; in contrast, the social model poses disability as multidimensional subjective identity, which is socially constructed as undesirable and marginalized by political and social systems in need of change. Duffy recalled her doctors and others talking about her as if she wasn't there, deciding her future without her consent. Such paternalistic voices echoing in Duffy's head were internalized, she explained, turning the performance into a coming out and claiming of the right to be seen as a political subject *and* a sexual being. She also expressed frustration with herself for previously giving in, for remaining invisible and silent, asserting: "I wasn't able to talk back." In this act of talking back, Duffy performed personal and social resistance. Duffy placed the performance in a series of actions that have confronted self-imposed shame, or what she deems her "inner monster." Making a spectacular spectacle of herself,

Duffy exposed her disabled female body, as well as the artistic and social traditions that have deemed it shameful and unacceptable. Duffy's self-exhibition is disarming. It allures, bewitches, and shocks viewers strategically, while it removes the defenses of both the performer and her audience. The performance exposes the nude disabled body visually and artistically, as it also reveals the social practices and values that render disability politically invisible. Duffy incarnates the Venus de Milo, an epitome of Western ideals for female artistic beauty; yet her body in live performance defies social standards of appearance acceptability. The performance alters perceptions of the body in representation and in society, as it links histories of female and disabled bodies on display.

In this chapter, I will place Duffy's performance in dialogues with related images of the female body drawn from histories of painting and sculpture, photography, and the freak show, arguing that languages of disability, such as those Duffy exposes, condemns, and reinvents, may tell alternative and potentially liberating narratives of representation. I characterize these images as Venuses to exhibit how the Venus tradition recycles across visual media and historical contexts and embodies confusions of conventional and anticonventional (i.e., subversive) forms of representation. Venuses display body ideals, as well as deviance. Because the Venus tradition is tied specifically to histories of representing the "other," my comparisons show how disability studies perspectives have been informed by and contribute to issues of race, gender, class, and sexuality in body criticism. Using Duffy's performance as a model, I read comparative images against the grain of, or in opposition to, repressive narratives of disability and of representation to disrupt them and to empower the subjects on display—the disarmed "others"—with performative agency, as these Venuses gaze and talk back. My comparison of Duffy's work with that of her contemporaries, other disabled or "disfigured" female artists who represent their own bodies, places this work into a history of art and performance. I argue that these artists' work, in the media of performance and performative photography, distinguishes itself from that of its foremothers (particularly feminist performance and body art of the 1970s onward), as it embodies and negotiates social forces that demonize disabled female bodies distinctively.

## Posing in/as the Nude

Duffy inserts her body into the tradition of the female nude from its Classical Western foundations, challenging body ideals. Her body recalls the Classical marble sculpture of the armless Venus de Milo, which viewers often accept as a broken relic. Art historian Kenneth Clark (1956) has called the Venus de Milo the greatest work of antiquity, arguing that such models set the precedent of ideal beauty throughout art history, as well as for other forms of visual culture.[3] Therefore, the Venus figure reappears across various art historical periods and visual media as an ideal that proves to be intricately deceptive. The Venus becomes a generic trope that aestheticizes and justifies voyeuristic and often problematic exploitations of the body, specifically through conventions which stage a female body as sexually available and complacent with her display. In the Venus tradition, the model becomes an object for visual consumption.

Predominant feminist theories of representation, drawn from psychoanalytic theories surrounding identity formation and look- ing at the "other," argue that the female nude represents not a real woman, but rather "Woman" as set of formal conventions—a symbol always mediated by the heterosexual, patriarchal gaze. Marina Warner (1985) explains that women in representation, from the earliest myths and histories, are conventionally ascribed meaning rather than empowered to make meaning, and that an image of a man is more often considered a portrait of a specific individual, whereas women's bodies are viewed as symbolic or as objects of fantasy.[4] This "Woman" in representation is an image of what the male creator lacks; she is objectified in the process of the assumed male viewer defining himself as everything she is not and in his potential dominance over and possession of her.[5] In other words, the image of "Woman" represents the desires and subjectiv- ity of those who produce it, rather than expressing anything about the identity of the body on display. Relating to Classical ideals and modern psychoanalytic elaborations, the female body in represen- tation is castrated to confirm the image-producer's masculinity, and therefore without her own agency. Thus, the Venus de Milo may be *the* ultimate representation of the female form, always lacking in some of the most visible body parts, visually and metaphorically disarmed. Duffy's defiantly subjective performance brings to life how the female form is always already impaired in its symbolic disempowerment and amputation, as she "disables" (i.e., impairs, yet also brings disability perspectives to) the ideal.

Duffy's performance also disables many theoretical notions of the gaze.[6] Due to pervasive voyeurism, women and all people with disabilities are objects of often exploitative gazes. Similarly to how representations of "Woman" eclipse the experience of real women, disability studies theorists, such as Rosemarie Garland-Thomson (1997; 2000; 2005; 2009) have argued that pervasive representations in culture often produce restrictive and stereotypical images of disability and erase disabled people as political and social subjects.

I recognize many of the similarities between the gaze and stare that Garland-Thomson articulates, yet I see more dimensions, particularly as they operate in visual culture. Garland-Thomson argues, for example, that photographs of people with disabilities provide a medium for the viewer to stare at a photographically produced "other." She maintains further that whereas live performances by disabled artists, such as Duffy, allow for progressive self-representation and returned stares;[7] photographs foreclose any dynamic exchange between the viewer and the body on display.[8] I extend her notions of live performance to interpret two-dimensional images, such as photographs and paintings, which I see as potentially performative. Looking at the "other" (for example a disabled individual) may be an attempt to define the self (to confirm the viewer's able-bodied "normalcy"), destabilizing notions of difference and distance between the viewer and the image. Further, one who looks may be caught in the act and subject to potentially transformative reactions, as the "other," such as Duffy, stares back, disarmingly.[9] Below, I engage ideas of reciprocal, dynamic gazes and stares in looking at a series of disarming Venus images.

Contemporary photographer Joel Peter Witkin's *First Casting for Milo* (2003) (featured on the cover of this book) showcases how the Venus figure emerges across multiple histories of visual culture. Witkin's work is controversial in his use of specifically anticonventional, anti-idealized bodies in excessive and taboo displays. One of his fascinations is amputees,[10] as featured in this black and white photograph of a woman with uniquely finger-free hands, posing on a stage in seductive lingerie and partially shrouding drapery.

The photograph captures the shimmering and luscious surfaces of this exotic beauty and her theatrical surroundings. This amputee Venus is a corporeal and symbolic beauty; she is a historical Classical sculpture in her first "casting," a term that enters into the languages of medicine, sculpture, and theater. The amputee is also "cast" as a Hollywood starlet, emphasized by her classical Hollywood coiffed hair, period bra, and the clichéd film slate and clapboard in the margins. She poses like a statue and silent film star, with specific reference to the Venus de Milo. The inclusion of a dog echoes conventional iconography in portrait painting, in which the dog is an elusive symbol of a female subject's sexuality, domestication, morality, and dominance over subordinate creatures. The dog is already a multivalent symbol in art history, and Witkin adds an additional, comic layer, for this "first casting" is, indeed, for *Milo*—a name that may refer to the dog rather than the female model. Confusions of iconography and genre drive the image and destabilize the viewer's assumptions when staring at disability. Further, Witkin's image is unconventional as a photographic portrait of a glamorous woman with exotic hands—a vision of desire for multiple gazes. Witkin's photograph, like Duffy's performance, inserts the disabled body into a dubious history of Venuses and starlets, yet it provides the female model a stage on which to perform as an object of desire.

*First Casting for Milo* increases the dimensions of gazing and staring at disability. Garland-Thomson (2001) and David Hevey (1998) have criticized photographs of visibly disabled people for directing the gaze toward and fetishizing impaired body parts (in this case, her unique hands), providing a medium that sanctions a problematic social stare.[11] Yet, voyeurism is inherent to the medium of photography in general and a power that may be employed for subversion. Witkin's staging of this amputee in the guise of multiple Venuses invites the stare to her so-called deformed hands, yet places them and the rest of her body in a context of theatrical enchantment and erotic imagery. It freezes in two dimensions the visual experience of staring at her hands, yet it also gives the viewer an excess of visual context and an excess of other visual pleasures to consume. The photograph causes viewers confusion about their own positions in their acts of looking. This image contains alternative narration, as it documents a potentially transgressive, perhaps self-empowering masquerade for the amputee model.

Performative stagings, such as Duffy's and Witkin's, turn the Venus tradition inside out and expose its conventions as deceptive. In this way, they follow in the "Venus" tradition of Édouard Manet's *Olympia* (1863). *Olympia*, modeled after Titian's *Venus of Urbino* (1538) and now itself a canonical masterpiece, subverted the Venus tradition, by calling attention to its inherent corruptions. Both works present the unclothed female body in an odalisque pose within a private room; however in Titian's painting a decorative chaise and a beguilingly posed, Rubenesque body has been replaced in Manet's version with a thinner and aesthetically flatter body, adorned with a suggestive flower in her hair, necklace, and high-heeled shoes. She occupies a bed within a setting that rejects traditional, illusionistic depiction of three-dimensional space, as seen in *Venus of Urbino*, and effectively pushes the naked body foreword, into the viewer's space. Further, *Olympia* was recognized as a modern prostitute rather than a strategically ambiguous and anonymous Venus, as in Titian's artful display of the nude. Art historian Timothy J. Clark (1992) maintains that *Olympia* deviated from norms for representing the female nude in art history, as she broke social codes for femininity and class.[12] The shocking qualities of the painting resulted from the nakedness and performative agency of her body, versus the conventionalized notion of a passive, artistic nude. The bodily transgressions of *Olympia* emerged in painterly hints at pubic hair and an aggressive hand covering her sex, or perhaps masturbating, as well as her confrontational returned gaze. *Olympia* subversively quoted the conventionalized original, pointing to the fact that the model of Titian's painting was likely also a "courtesan," rather than a generic nude or domesticated lover. In dialogue with *Olympia*, the *Venus of Urbino* proves erotic, perhaps pornographic despite her conventional, passive pose, so-called demure hand shielding her sex, and placement against a mythical landscape and in an upper-class boudoir (with inclusion of a chest that signifies her promise to marriage). Focusing on Titian's painting, art historian Rona Goffen (1997) explains how such iconography surrounding the female nude in art, even (or especially) in the most conventional of representations, is necessarily contradictory.[13] Others have framed the work as disarming in its illusionistic depiction of skin,[14] as conventions that mediate the female body on display fail to contain connotations of the flesh.

*Olympia* proved most transgressive in her body type. Clark postulates that *Olympia* "refuses to signify,"[15] highlighting the formal qualities of the painting and its subversively antiacademic, modernist aesthetic. It was her physical form, in other words, that was most disarming and subversive; Clark writes that Olympia's "incorrectness" in rendering led viewers to remark on her "physical deformity."[16] In these examples, critics engaged languages of disability to characterize *Olympia*'s defiance of artistic conventions as well as her breach of class boundaries in nineteenth-century France. Like Duffy, this Venus placed itself into a tradition and mocked it with physical departures from the norm. These Venuses destabilize their viewers due to their intense corporealities and disarming returned gazes.[17]

These two- and three-dimensional performances expose how the Venus tradition has attempted to justify profoundly exploitative displays of the female body historically, as exemplified by the phenomenon of the "Hottentot Venus." Saartjie Baartman was taken from the "Hottentot" people of Africa's Ivory Coast[18] in the nineteenth century and put on public display in London as a savage, oversexualized "Hottentot" Venus. Baartman's body on display, like Duffy's, solicited a gaze/stare tainted with desire *and* repulsion, for she was staged as monstrous and classified as part ape in contemporary scientific and racist discourse.[19] Like Duffy, Baartman was victimized by science and medicine. The "Hottentot Venus" became a medical specimen/erotic spectacle that was racially, sexually, and brutally objectified under the guise of scientific objectivity: posthumously, Baartman was dissected and her remains were placed on display in the Musée de l'Homme in Paris, until only recently.[20] The "Hottentot Venus" illustrates a manipulation of the Venus tradition, used to mediate the objectification and violence (dissection, dehumanization) against the female body across various forms of visual culture.

Public displays and numerous illustrations of Baartman's body crossed genres of medical, artistic, and popular (spectacle and pornographic) imagery, such that the Hottentot Venus was constructed by multiple gazes and stares. Historian Sander Gilman (1986) expounds upon how the visual image of the "Hottentot" became an iconic symbol for *all* black women as hypersexual, primitive, and monstrous.[21] Gilman draws comparisons to popular images and the inclusions of ambiguous black figures in paintings such as *Olympia*. Visual representations of Baartman portrayed her deviance physiognomically in profile exaggerations of her "Hottentot" physique (excessive, or more ample than "normal," i.e., White Victorian, derriere and genitals). Gilman argues this image of deviance served as an example against which white Victorian culture established their identities as normal and civilized. Parallels may be drawn to Duffy's experiences of being "othered" by medical and social gazes to affirm the normalcy of those who stare.

This comparison links racist and ableist discourses further, for Baartman's "abnormality," like *Olympia*'s, was framed through languages of disability.[22] Baartman, and the black women she represented, were deemed abnormal and thus pathologically deviant based on the evidence of "deformed" anatomy. Phrenologist and eugenicist Cesare Lombroso argued that genital differences, or specifically "deformities," in Hottentots were characteristic of less evolved races and degenerate criminal types.[23] Lombroso's practice, phrenology, involved the measuring and mapping of anatomies to determine individuals of "higher" and "lower" evolution, and therefore intelligence. Within the phrenological, Positivist discourses of the nineteenth century, white Victorians were differentiated from racial and corporeal "others," such as Baartman and the black, animalistic women she came to exemplify, through specifically visual practices and displays. Images of Baartman fetishized her so-called abnormal body parts in pseudo-objective, scientific renderings, as they mediated staring at the deformed and uncivilized "other." Baartman's so-called impairments, perhaps not so impairing in the eyes of the heterosexual, patriarchal gaze, were the visual evidence of a deviant woman. Baartman's stage name as a "Venus" was invoked to justify her display and proved ironic, for the Classical body was the basis for constructing its supposed binary opposite, the bestial, primitive body. Interrogating the "Hottentot Venus" through lenses of disability adds layers of significance, as images of Venuses throughout history become more disarming in comparison.

Contemporary African-American photographer Renée Cox employs disarming self-exhibition, similarly to Duffy, as she performs in her photographs as female personas drawn from art history and popular culture (the Madonna, *Olympia*, and a superhero, for examples), many of which are pseudopornographic. Cox's images parody long histories of exploitation, eroticization, and visual stereotyping of the black female body specifically, in excessive poses of sexual availability. In *HOT-EN-TOT* (1994), Cox impersonates the "Hottentot Venus" in a profile view (a physiognomic trope), which accentuates her curves, made exaggeratedly theatrical with the use of prosthetics—costume breasts and buttocks that mimic the clichéd reduction of woman to tits and ass. The image calls attention to the contrived nature of her historical model; the "Hottentot Venus" proves to be pure image—a complete fabrication in historical imagination and significance. Therefore, images of the "Hottentot Venus" provide no information about Baartman as a historical individual, but rather, they depict the abusive desires of her spectators. Perhaps problematically, Cox's version erases the violence embedded in its nineteenth-century precedents. Embodying the "Hottentot Venus," Cox makes Baartman more human, recognized as a contemporary social subject in a color photograph, and so affirmatively "Cox" in her made up hair and face, which returns an assertive gaze. Simultaneously, Cox's costumed version disarmingly portrays Baartman as pure persona and cultural myth. Cox constructs a Hottentot likeness that attempts to mock those who produced and consumed such images, yet fails to give Baartman a voice to talk back.

Cox, posing as a historical freak and contemporary photographic spectacle, interrogates the potential agency, as well as dangers, of exhibitionism. The history of freak displays raises a variety of parallels between cultural forms of objectifying certain "abnormal" bodies—raced, disabled, and hypersexualized, for examples, and provides a wealth of visual materials that produced those bodies as "others." During their heyday of popular entertainment in the United States (c. 1840–1940), freak show displays and the numerous two-dimensional images generated from them exploited the gaze/stare at disability. The freak show functioned on and magnified the status of disabled people as social outcasts. Cartes de visites of freak show performers, postcard-sized collectible photographs, became wildly popular during the late nineteenth century. Among politicians, war heroes (many amputees), obscene attractions, and celebrities, freak show performers became public personalities in their cartes de visite images—armless wonders in particular would often autograph them with a footprint. The most famous showman of all time, P. T. Barnum, hired photographers to produce marketing and souvenir portraits of his casts of human curiosities. With particular relevance to the theme of disarming Venuses, Ann E. Leak-Thompson was one of many amputees staged by the freak show as armless and legless wonders, miraculous "half" people and unbelievable human torsos (Figure 1.1). She was also featured in collectible souvenir photographs, which become part of the historical representation of disability as freakish spectacle. In dialogue with performances of other Venuses in this paper, photographs of Leak-Thompson push further frameworks of disability as performatively staged.

Such publicity photographs capitalized on portraying disability as sensational and sentimental. Examples by Charles Eisenmann purport Leak-Thompson's morality to her patrons in their photographic compositions.[24] She is staged as a proper Victorian lady who performs domestic crafts, as suitable for the female social role. The photograph is conventionalized in a black and white, nineteenth-century family portrait style, as Leak-Thompson is surrounded by props that identify and label her for the viewer and is dressed in proper Victorian dress. Specifically, the setting asserts Leak-Thompson's status as a wife and mother, marked as extraordinary or different from the status quo by her bare feet, one holding scissors. Repeated inclusions in her portraits of embroidery and crochet displaying Christian symbols and phrases, as well as moralistic quotes on the back of the photographs, emphasized her piety. Yet her "normalcy" is made extraordinary. Freak show displays commonly and condescendingly exalted disabled "freaks" for performing mundane tasks, as if the nonimpaired audiences could not fathom functioning with bodies different from their own. Domestic settings and props, which suggested Leak-Thompson's adaptive ability to be "normal," allowed viewers to identify with Leak-Thompson, while her undeniably abnormal body assured distance between the nondisabled spectators and the disabled spectacle. Her freak show biography, a characteristic hybrid of medical diagnosis and fantastical myth, emphasized that her birth defects resulted from the immorality of her parents: the "cause" of Anne's armless form was a result, according to her biography, of her mother witnessing her father coming home from a night of drinking and wearing a coat draped over his shoulders. Anne's mother, confused by

**Figure 1.1** Charles Eisenmann, *Armless Wonder.* Ann E Leake-Thompson (1884)

vision of her neglectful husband with no arms, was afflicted by maternal impressions that altered Anne's body. This narrative, based on contemporary pseudoscientific discourse and fantastical legend, communicated further to the patron voyeurs that Leake-Thompson's life took a deviant path because of the cross she had to bear in her armlessness. Therefore, audiences were encouraged to stare, as she had no viable alternatives than to perform for them, which further appeased any guilt. Despite efforts to normalize her, Leak-Thompson's live and photographic performances departed from the nineteenth-century standards of social respectability, because of her profession, as well as her body.

The freak show serves as an archive of and visual legacy for performances of disability. It staged Leake-Thompson's everyday life as a spectacle, relating to Duffy's experiences of being stared at and asked inappropriate questions about her body and daily activities. Yet, viewing disability as freakishly performative, as in the photograph of Leake-Thomson and other visual images, raises complicated issues; performing, in the experiences of people with disabilities, may be an obligation, burden, and/or a tool, as well as an exercise of agency. Questions surrounding the ultimate consequences of self-exhibition are particularly layered for those who are displayed sometimes against their will and simultaneously politically invisible; yet in Duffy's example, performance as a freakish Venus becomes a means to intrude upon and liberate herself from histories of oppressive representations of women and disabled women specifically. Through her performative work, we may transgressively re-interpret convention and unpack historical representation, in a revision of art history. Part of this interventionist work involves looking closer, staring, seeing from multiple perspectives, and disarming the conventional staging, as well as the conventional reading, of images.

## Disfiguring Histories of Performance

Feminist theories of representation and forms of embodied activism, particularly feminist performance art, set the stage for Duffy's and other disabled and "disfigured" artists' contemporary work. Feminist performance art flourished in the 1970s as part of the feminist art movement, a revival of traditionally feminine crafts and practices, as well as movements for feminist rights and theory. Artists such as Carolee Schneemann, Hannah Wilke, Adrian Piper, Eleanor Antin, Karen Finley, Valie Export, Gina Pane, Yayoi Kusama, and others[25] performed before audiences and cameras, often in the nude, to celebrate the female body and reclaim it from multiple histories of objectification. These artists deconstructed historical representation of female body in art, such as in the Venus tradition, and in popular culture. By revealing their bodies and using their bodies as a stage or a canvas, these performers exposed how art history has depended on sexual exploitation and often violence against female body, while it has erased female subjectivity.[26] Rejecting masculine-biased trends in art history, such as formalism, aesthetic disinterest, and commodification of the art object, these feminists used their bodies as art to upset the status quo.

While feminist performance waned in impact over the decade, and in the eyes of many became absurd, the work broke ground for other minority artists who battled the same biases in the history of art and asserted their social visibility. Manet's *Olympia*, for example, has been quoted subversively by a number of contemporary artists, such as in the photographs of Cox, Japanese artist Yasimasa Morimura, and live performances of Carolee Schneemann (with Robert Morris). These pieces interrogate images of "Woman," social constructions of gender and race, and objectifying practices of visual culture. Such works portray the notion of identity as largely a surface performance, with their particularly performative gestures of self-display and masquerade. The work of disabled artists, such as Mary Duffy, Petra Kuppers, Carrie Sandahl, Cheryl Marie Wade, and Sally Banes, is rooted in the feminist art movement and its legacy for contemporary performance and photography, yet their work distinguishes itself as more particularized to their unique bodies and body histories: (a)sexual, medical, and often shameful histories. Duffy's work utilizes what performance scholar Rebecca Schneider has termed the "explicit body" in performance—a literal, material body that complicates purely symbolic or idealized forms of the female body, particularly those offered by the traditions of the nude. These bodies, like Duffy's, disrupt social perceptions of body standards and assert their visible, tangible corpo*realities*, as well as their subjective bodily experiences. Many disabled and "disfigured" artists invest their work with individual and uniquely embodied experiences. These artists' works frame their particularized histories of marginalization, objectification, and social rejection, histories which are still largely invisible to mainstream culture.

The performance and bodywork of many female artists with disabilities intervene on histories of representing women's bodies, while targeting the stigma and shame imposed on the disabled female body specifically. Whereas much feminist-inspired performance and body art has objected to displays of the female body as a site of infinite desire and possession, Duffy confronts a sexual economy from which her body has been excluded, rejected, and made freakish. Duffy explains how she has been made to feel physically and sexually inadequate or damaged, causing shameful body images and, consequently, both her self- and socially imposed invisibility. Through displaying her explicit body, Duffy reclaims her right to be seen naked while posing in the nude, as she provides a particular confusion the naked/nude dyad. The nude is poignantly an idealized form and is often falsely differentiated from the state of being naked,[27] which is associated with shame and with a real body or social subject exposed for the scrutiny of the gaze/stare, as well as with a medical specimen. Warner (1985) and others have interrogated these cultural oppositions of the nude and the naked, pointing out how the naked body in representation may signify a lack of moral concern and sinful behavior, and yet such shamelessness may also suggest a freedom from shame or a state of unashamed truth.[28]

The naked, shameless body, like Duffy's, may reject the very pretenses of nude versus naked. In an earlier performance titled *Stories of the Body* (1990), commissioned by and performed at the Rochdale Art Gallery in Manchester, United Kingdom, Duffy delivered a monologue similar to her 1995 performance in Michigan; she spoke about her experiences as a disabled woman and artist, particularly about feeling corporeally shamed, desexualized, and dehumanized through diagnosing gazes, intrusive questions, and demeaning assumptions. Also like her 1995 performance, Duffy performed completely nude. In *Stories of the Body* Duffy additionally projected slide images onto her body as she spoke to create visually the experience of how the media constructs demeaning images of disability, which are projected onto her body in everyday social encounters. She chose to be nude in these performances to explore the vast dimensions and dynamics of voyeurism. Her photographic series *Cutting the Ties that Bind* (1987), commissioned by Arts Council of Ireland, features Duffy again as the Venus, progressively removing or losing her Classical drapery covering.[29] These eight photographs are accompanied by text that relates similar discourse as her live performances in poetic verse. Throughout her work, Duffy personifies the cultural symbol of the Venus de Milo in the flesh, while speaking about her particularized, embodied experiences. This body on display overturns perceptions of art and of bodies as "whole" versus deficient.

Duffy is unique, but not alone. Below I draw thematic and visual comparisons between Duffy's performance and the work of other female artists who feature their "disfigured" and explicit bodies in performative, photographic displays. I compare Duffy's self-images with those of Sandie Yi, Cheryl Marie Wade, Susan Harbage Page, and Hannah Wilke, in order to place the works within a context of contemporary art. These artists' body artworks engage interactive and performative exchanges of gazes and stares in their discovery of self-images.

## Self-Imaging

Duffy's performance embodies her history as a disabled female. Likewise, other contemporary artists expose their disabled or "disfigured" bodies in performative self-representations to confront stigma, manipulate the gaze, and cleanse shame. Taiwanese born artist Sandie Yi photographs herself wearing accessories self-fashioned for her unique physique (Figure 1.2). Yi's mixed-media, handmade bracelets, gloves, and shoes serve as adornments and protection for her two-fingered hands and two-toed feet, the sites of her impairments, as well as features that have been the target for social stigma and startled, often horrified stares. Her photographic series *Armed and Beautiful* (2005) features the artist showcasing her feet, which she characteristically hides from public view, modeling self-crafted high heels. High heels are, in the realm on consumer culture, a female fetish and obsession that signify the display of feminine beauty and sexual availability. In the vernacular of fashion, Yi's shoes are strappy sandals with stacked, chunky heels; yet they appear prehistoric rather than trendy with their rocky, jagged platforms, and fierce horns, which protrude from between Yi's two toes to "arm" her.

**Figure 1.2**　Sandie Yi, *Armed and Beautiful* (2005). Photographed by Cheng-Chang Kuo

The precarious balance offered by the heel height and shape, as well as the illusion of a foot split into two by the shoes' design, reference visually the footbinding practices of Yi's Chinese heritage (which Yi acknowledges but did not necessarily intend), a historic ritual in which women's feet were painfully stunted in development and consequentially immobilized for the purpose of beauty. These practices combine culturally specific standards for feminine beauty, and the consequential, often radical body alterations imposed to achieve them, with physical impairment; footbinding "beautifies" while effectively disfiguring and disabling female bodies. In *Armed and Beautiful*, Yi rescues these histories as well as her personal histories of being made to feel unattractive and unfeminine due to her so-called disfigurements, here made beautiful through display in artful, photographic aesthetics. Her contorted and seductive pose in skintight pants, which titillates the viewer by concealing her bare breast, perhaps dubiously exoticizes the Asian female body; the photographs provide a medium to gaze and stare, yet capture the viewer's visual attention in Yi's own terms. The shoes and the photographs stage Yi as beautiful, sexy, and foremost, armed and empowered to combat stigma. In comparison with Duffy as a revealing Venus, Yi becomes Athena, the Greek and Roman goddess of wisdom, war, the arts, and dualities (war and peace, male and female). Athena was further the protector of women and women's work, which in Yi's narrative, become female self-beautifying rituals, ancient and contemporary. Her two toes on each self-fetishized feet are decorously exposed and armed against shame.

Cheryl Marie Wade, a wheelchair-user with "clawlike" hands, writes and performs poetry and witty commentary on her experiences as a disfigured woman in contemporary society. Her poems include *I Am Not One of The* and *Cripple Lullaby*.[30] Wade's multidimensional role in disability culture encompasses work as a visual artist, performer, poet, and disability rights activist (especially against the right-to-die movement), and she is first disabled woman to win the NEA (The National Endowment for the Arts) grant. Her performance art, more so than Duffy's, transgresses the frame of visual art into theater and "stand-up" (here, seated) comedy. Wade created and starred in a one-woman show called *Sassy Girl: Memoirs of a Poster Child Gone Awry*,[31] which opened in 1994 at Brava Theater Center in San Francisco, and later toured to other cities. In 1985,

Wade also founded *Wry Crips*, a theatrical medium for California women with disabilities to perform poems, skits, and dramatic readings about their bodies and the role of their bodies in their lives, like Duffy's performance. Her multimedia, multidimensional work meshes autobiography, performance, literature, and personal narrative, a form that has been widely embraced and produced in disability studies as a discipline and disability rights movements to combat false social stereotypes and mainstream ignorance about disabled people. The personal storytelling performs the explicit body, as she parodies her experiences with stigma and shame from the medical profession and society at large.

Like the model in Witkin's *First Casting for Milo* and Yi, Wade's most visible impairment are her disfigured hands, and like the two-dimensional photographs that feature *Milo* and Yi, Wade's poems and performances draw visual attention to and self-narrative her hands. Wade's hands become central to both her social identity and marginalization, because of their deformity, and many might say, freakish ugliness. Particularly in the following spoken-word performance, *My Hands*, Wade frames her hands as a source of impairment, exploitative cultural display (by medicine and charity), and stigma. At the same time, her hands are a source of artistic creation, subversive power, and desirability:

> Mine are the hands of your bad dreams
> boogabooga from behind the black curtain
> claw hands, the ivory girl's hands
> after a decade of roughing it.
> Crinkled, puckered, sweaty, scared, a young girl's dwarf, knobby hands
> that ache from moonlight,
> that tremble—that struggle.
> Hands that make your eyes tear
> My hands, my hands, my hands
> That could grace your brow, your thighs
> My hands.
> Yea![32]
> (transcription mine)

Wade performs in multiple and transgressive roles in this self-portrait piece. She morphs from a creature of horror and magic ("hands that make your eyes tear" and "boogabooga, behind the black curtain"), the latter, a reference that could also allude to the freak show; to an animal ("claw hands"), to a contemporary, working class woman ("after a decade of roughing it"), specifically an impaired one ("that tremble—that struggle"; "dwarf, knobby hands"); and to a historical temptress and contemporary, disabled sexual being ("my hands that could grace your brow, your thighs"). In performing the last few lines of the poem, Wade places different emphasis on the repetition of "my hands"—the first somewhat defensive, the next self-affirming and unashamed, and the final, pressing the envelope further, with suggestive intonation and provocative facial expression. Here, the power of sexuality for the so-called disfigured woman becomes alluringly sexy and playfully deviant. Her fantastical roles span a human/animal monster with "clawed" hands to a seductive, fairy-tale siren; Warner (1985) has described sirens as mermaidlike femme fatales in Classical mythology, who lured sailors with their voices, lulled them to sleep, and then sneaked on board to tear them to pieces.[33] In acts of destruction, language is the sirens' weapon. In these examples, Wade's self-narration subverts and reclaims language that conventionally subjugates and objectifies, as well as the power dynamics of the gaze/stare. In her poem *I Am Not One of The*, Wade also asserts: "I'm a sock in the eye with a gnarled fist," which Garland-Thomson (2000) has interpreted as a confrontational, returned gaze by the disabled spectacle[34]—establishing a two-directional gaze with and from a visually disfigured and stigmatized body. Wade empowers her role as a woman who defies, even actively refuses to conform to social standards for women's bodies and conventional cultural displays of them.

Contemporary artist Susan Harbage Page's photographs similarly defy social standards for and conventional representations of women's bodies (Figure 1.3). Like Duffy's and Wade's self-mediations, Page's self-portrait photographs assert the anti-ideal. These images embody multiple histories of Page's own personal body (her explicit body), as well as women's bodies everywhere: body histories of desire, shame, fear, pain, stigma, dismemberment, and reconstruction. Page's photographs embody her battles with breast cancer and frame Audre Lorde's (1984) articulation that the shared experiences of breast cancer bring women of all

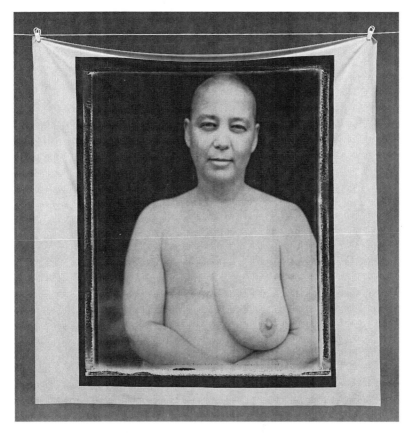

**Figure 1.3**   Susan Harbage Page, *A Question of Beauty* (2000)

corporealities and races together.[35] Page's self-portrait from the waist up, *A Question of Beauty* (2000) reveals her nude torso with one breast and a postmastectomy scar. Beneath her baldhead (a result of chemotherapy), her face bears little expression, neither inviting nor deterring the viewer's gaze/stare at her body, marked by cancer and consequential emotional battles. The question asked by the photograph is what defines femininity and beauty, particularly for women, or even appearance acceptability. Conversely, the image asks what characterizes a defeminized or "damaged" body. Hair, particularly long hair, signifies feminine beauty and youth for women, and Page has been mistaken for a man after losing her hair. The breast signifies an even greater range of characteristics associated with femininity. The naked breast, most frequently fetishized on the female body to eroticize and objectify it for the heterosexual male gaze, may be a source of shame for the woman, when revealed for social or medical scrutiny or when she has been made to feel physically inadequate due to the shape, size, or absence of breasts, and therefore considered undesirable. The breastless woman, such as Page and other cancer survivors, likewise face shame and stigma against their "diseased" and "disfigured" bodies. Further, women's breasts bear multiple personal significances; Page has remarked on how in youth, breasts represent a girl's development of woman-hood and sexual desirability, while later they provide sustenance and nurturing to children, and then, when faced with breast cancer, the breasts transform from life-givers to life-takers and the source of pain. Removal of the breast therefore is a simultaneous loss and relief. Both the breast present and the one absent in Page's photo-graphs represent the process of the body's aging and its inevitable vulnerability, states of the body for which women especially feel ashamed in contemporary culture's obsession with youth and impossible standards for bodily "perfection."

Page's work resonates with Hannah Wilke's photographs of her own breast cancer, which, in comparison with her earlier feminist performance work, underscore the unique materialization of the disabled or disfigured body in visual images. Wilke's photographic self-portrait series performed at the end of her life, *Intra-Venus* (a collaboration with Donald Green) (c. 1993) documents Wilke's body dying of cancer. The images recreate many of the composi-tions of her earlier 1970s work, which featured Wilke, often topless, in the exaggerated poses of conventionalized and commercialized female roles, such as the odalisque, shrouded "oriental" woman, Hollywood glamour girl, pinup girl, stripper (making parodies of the removal of clothing), and the pornographic model, in a "bea-ver shot." These poses appear most comprehensively in Wilke's *S.O.S.—Starification Object Series* (1974). Wilke was heavily criti-cized for simply recommodifying and objectifying her own body, because she was a young and conventionally sexy woman, and thus her images invited the heterosexual male gaze. In intentional contrast, the *Intra-Venus* series makes Wilke's poses disarming in the graphic display of bodily carnality, which proves to often be not pretty. Wilke's once glorious, long hair (again, a sign of youth and femininity) is lost through chemotherapy, and the clothes that barely cover here are a surgical gown and hospital slippers. The body in these images is intensely carnal, aged, disfigured, and medicalized, and the photographs threaten the viewer with remembrance of mortality and the pervasive disease of cancer. The title *Intra-Venus* invokes the medical term for surgical procedures and chemotherapy treatments specifically, in which the body is injected with "curing" poisons, as well as the Venus tradition of displaying the nude, idealized female body. Wilke's body of work questions the importance of beauty for women and the effects of a disease specific to women's bodies, similarly to Page's work.

As seen in the work of Duffy, Yi, Wade, and Wilke, Page impersonates mythical and goddess imagery to perform a self-defined, powerful body image. Page's photographs of her own and other women's bodily histories are heavily inspired by art historical representations of the Virgin Mary. Page is fascinated by Catholicism's reverence of empowered female saints, particularly healing saints, who serve as the protectors of women and women's bodies. Her steely returned gaze in *A Question of Beauty* challenges the viewer to really *see* the effects of breast cancer, yet the image can only show the surface of her particular experiences. She printed this image on semitransparent silk to reference veils, which appear in many of her works. A similar self-portrait with a bald head appears in a diptych, paired with an image of a woman wearing a black shador veil; both images are out of focus and printed on silk to underscore themes concealing, indicated by the diptych's title, *You Still Can't See Me* (2000). This work was displayed in *Still Standing* at the ATA Center for Contemporary Art in Sofia, Bulgaria in 2001 along with Page's photographs, also blurry, of veiled women across the world (nuns in Italy and Arab women in purdah, for examples). These images suggest the inherent dynamics within all photographs between what is revealed and what remains veiled. *You Still Can't See Me* exemplifies the potential power of withholding images of the body from the economy of visual exploitation, and the photographs' elusiveness frame how all representations fail to capture the "whole" of a subject and the subject's relationships with their body. As perhaps best articulated by Phelan (1993), images always suggest an excess that the viewer's eye cannot see—a simultaneous presence and absence of a body within and beyond the frame. Phelan further explains the interconnectedness between mediums of live performance, such as

Duffy's, and photography (as in the work of Yi, Lapper, Wilke, and Page), for the tangible "liveness" of photography and its theatrical posturing, staging, and strategic construction make it performative, particularly in self-portraiture.

## Interacting with the Body

Duffy's and these photographers' bodies transcend the stages of art and everyday life through embodied performance. They showcase the disabled, disfigured, and stigmatized body as performative. I term Duffy's performance of disability as interacting, in continuous negotiations of inner and outer images of the self, as well as continuous exchanges with others who stare. Duffy's work, for me, epitomizes a movement in the work of disabled artists and activists who showcase performance as personally and politically potent; such performances may be viewed on the video *Vital Signs: Crip Culture Talks Back* and *Shameless: The Art of Disability*.[36] Duffy's performance is an exorcism of inner demons, an absolving of shame, as she displays a self-defined and empowered body image of subject "wholeness." She asserts her bodily deviance from social standards to shake notions of ideals and norms to the core.

Duffy's disarming Venus performance serves as a legacy for landmark expressions of the disabled body. During the middle of the first decade of the twenty-first century, the citizens of London and its many visitors could step right up to the fourth plinth in Trafalgar Square to stare up at a monumental marble sculpture, by British artist Marc Quinn, of London resident, the amputee wonder Alison Lapper (see Figure 2.1). Lapper appeared in all her glory—nude and seven months pregnant. This image of Lapper, which opens Chapter 2, has raised much controversy and debates about the symbolic meanings of disability in visual culture and everyday social life, while making a public statement about Lapper's rights to be publicly visible as a sexual being and mother-to-be. The sculpture becomes, like Duffy's and other relevant artists' work, an interactive, public performance of disability. Perhaps due to controversy, the sculpture has brought global attention to Lapper's body, her life story, and her own artwork, predominantly decorative landscape paintings and assertive, photographic self-portraits. Lapper's own artistic interests in the human figure once focused on nondisabled bodies, as was the norm in art schools, until she was challenged to confront her body, both in her life and in her artwork. She was inspired to come out and expose herself socially and artistically by none other than a photograph of the Venus de Milo. In the pubic sculpture, Lapper, as a Venus, stares back at a public that has both welcomed and shunned her. Through shameless self-exhibition, Lapper, Duffy, and the work of relevant artists enact a revision of art history and sculpt new languages and representations for disability in the public eye.

# 2

# Sculpting Body Ideals

British citizen Alison Lapper was thrust into fame when her 11.5 foot tall, 13 ton sculptural portrait likeness, *Alison Lapper Pregnant*, was unveiled on the fourth plinth of Trafalgar Square in 2006, where it reigned for eighteen months (Figure 2.1). Lapper agreed to being cast in the nude by British artist Marc Quinn when she was seven months pregnant and to be placed on public display; many have called the project collaborative. The controversial sculpture has brought widespread attention to the model's body and her life story. Lapper, born without arms and with shortened legs, is an alumnus of British institutions for disabled children and programs for disabled artists, now a single mother, and an artist who makes work about her body and embodied experiences as a disabled woman. Carved from precious Italian marble and placed on a pedestal among statues of British naval captains, Lapper has been called a contemporary heroine of cultural diversity. Deemed by some as "brave and bold" and "pregnant and proud" and by others as a tasteless and overtly political publicity stunt for Quinn, the work makes a public statement about disability and Lapper's right to be seen as a productive social subject *and* a reproductive sexual being. The exposure of Lapper's body transcends the fact that she is nude, for Lapper grew up in the insolated environments of public intuitions and had limited interactions with public life; for Lapper, the work is a true coming out. The monumental sculpture and Lapper's own self-portrait photography become displays of the disabled body that transgress public and private realms and bear implications for individual and social bodies.

**Figure 2.1**  Marc Quinn, *Alison Lapper Pregnant* (2005)

This chapter will interrogate the sculpture's representation of disability within the contexts of Trafalgar Square the genre of Public Art, as well as in comparison with Lapper's self-representations. *Alison Lapper Pregnant* is a successful work of public art, based on the criteria that public art should respond to as well as transform the history of its particular space and interact with the populations who inhabit that space. The work plays with the highly idealizing themes and visual forms of public statuary and other Neoclassical works. Like Duffy's performance, it also challenges perceptions of amputated, sculptural bodies as "whole" or "broken," which bring into this analysis Quinn's many previous marble sculptures of amputees, from his series *The Complete Marbles*. *Alison Lapper Pregnant*, however, intensifies issues pertinent to *The Complete Marbles*, in its expanded proportions. As a monumental body and public spectacle, it recycles and contemporizes the representation of disability as both heroic and freakish, thus making stereotypes of and assumptions about disability visible and open for public debate. The work proves to be as dynamic and dialectical as the public itself, as I will illustrate through quoting a number of reactions to the sculpture by a range of viewers, drawn from public statements from sponsors, the artist (Quinn), and art critics; letters to the editor from the general public; and Lapper herself. The imposing sculpture poignantly brings into high relief contrasting discourses and assumptions about disabled bodies in cultural representation by forging important debates. Lapper's photography and her recently published memoir are key components of such discussions, as they provide perspectives by and a voice to the disabled subject on display. By weaving together these contexts of and reactions to Quinn's and Lapper's works, this chapter underscores the necessity of placing the works of disabled and nondisabled artists in dialogues with one another and with larger histories of visual culture.

## Art in the Public Eye

Public art brings to the fore issues of social and artistic representation and the visibility and invisibility of certain members of society. It demands an interdisciplinary, visual and social analysis, for it marks the intersections between artistic and social representation and the constructions of social space. Public space and its monuments have been gendered male and raced white traditionally, and public space is largely ableist in attitude, not to mention accessibility (or lack thereof). Public art, when the most effective, creates dialogues about the roles of art in society and who is included and excluded in the notion of the "public." It is in this context that *Alison Lapper Pregnant* performs its social work.

Found in spaces of both leisure and commerce, public art projects traditionally purport to create a harmonious community, increase tourism, and humanize and beautify space. In the 1980s and 1990s in the United Kingdom, where *Alison Lapper Pregnant* resides, many public art projects were funded as part of larger initiatives for urban renewal and life enhancement.[1] Public commissions for open air murals and sculpture consequentially increased, setting the stage for the Fourth Plinth program of Trafalgar Square, initiated in 1999.[2] Public arts training programs also developed, such as the ones that Lapper attended. These initiatives led to a flourishing of the arts and were based on the assumptions that art had inherent social and educational value. These public art projects were thought to have "civilizing" effects by creating social harmony, but also by leveling inherent public differences, tensions, and exclusions. Meant to appeal to the broadest notion of "public," publicly funded works were not meant to be largely critical or controversial and were constructed to produce economic, environmental, and social benefits, according to dominant social values and therefore following in the traditions of public monuments. Social geographer Malcolm Miles (1997) explains that "[m]onuments are produced within a dominant framework of values, as elements in the construction of a national history. . . . [T]hey suppose at least partial consensus of values, without which their narrative could not be recognized."[3] Monuments have portrayed political stability and stasis historically, rather than reflecting social change. Further, Miles underscores that monuments are versions and visual mediations of history, specifically ones constructed by those in power. Monuments often refer specifically to acts that have enforced that power, such as wars, conquest, conversion, colonialism, and violence, and therefore monuments legitimize power and its enforcement visually.

Yet more contemporary initiatives have contradicted such historical bases. In the spirit of civil rights and decolonization movements, as well as postmodernism, such monumental histories were largely contested from the 1980s onward. Many challenged the notion that "public" art was socially inclusive, as political movements protested the assumed neutrality of art and its expression of ideology. Many minority groups demanded representation and a redress of conventional biases in public art along gender, ethnic, and class lines. Including disability rights and arts programs, these initiatives demanded that public art represent diversity by engaging nontraditional art forms and by embodying multiculturalism. Honoring individuals marginalized and erased by dominant values and the structures that memorialize them, many contemporary public art projects have explicitly protested the status quo. These projects attempt to capture the tensions and dynamism of the contemporary urban population, and are intended to create not just dialogues, but controversy. This "new genre" of public art, as art critic Suzanne Lacy (1995) has termed it,[4] encompasses social and performative interactions between art and the public and demands the decolonization of public spaces. These public art forms, in which I contextualize *Alison Lapper Pregnant*, embody cultural battles for and of representation.

The sculpture produces Lapper as a representative of the historically underrepresented. Lapper has positioned the work at the forefront of such initiatives, stating: "I regard it as a modern tribute to femininity, disability and motherhood."[5] Here, she characterizes her body as a form of antimonument, for it represents the "other" to traditional subjects of public monuments, as well as an anti-ideal—a disruption of social standards for bodies and physical beauty. She acknowledges how her body becomes a monument to and for bodies and identities that have been historically and socially devalued, marginalized, and shamed. Specifically, women, mothers, and disabled people have all been largely excluded from public life. Lapper goes on in the same quote to note: "It is so rare to see disability in everyday life—let alone naked, pregnant and proud. The sculpture makes the ultimate statement about disability—that it can be as beautiful and valid a form of being as any other."[6]

Positive feedback about the sculpture also champions it as a liberating anti-ideal. For example, Bert Massie, the chairman of the commission, was quoted in the *Guardian* newspaper as stating: "Congratulations to Marc for realising that disabled bodies have a power and beauty rarely recognised in an age where youth and 'perfection' are idolised." This article also states that the Disability Rights Commission welcomed the statue as a source of pride and a blow against the cult of perfection that effectively disables bodies who don't conform to the norm.[7] Others have suggested, like Lapper, that the work's depiction of a specific embodiment largely underrepresented in visual life, at least in a positive way, broadens and humanizes notions of beauty, as well as humanizes certain socially stigmatized individuals.[8] The work may function to force the viewer to question their perceptions of the "ideal," and yet also question whose ideals Lapper is purported to represent.

## Classical Beauty

The work functions visually on the confusions between the ideal and the anti-ideal. Quinn's work is specifically a quotation of Neoclassicism, an eighteenth- and nineteenth-century European philosophy and artistic style (found in architecture, painting, sculpture, and the decorative arts) that championed reason, science, and morality in visual simplicity and heroic grandeur. Particularly in the contexts of the French Revolution, Neoclassicism extolled the artistic forms of empirical Rome and the tenants of Roman Republicanism. Neoclassical artists were academically trained about canonical masterpieces and pursued intellectual themes according to strict artistic conventions. Some of the better-known artists of this style are the French painter Jacques-Louis David, as well as the British painters Joshua Reynolds and Benjamin West, and the sculptors Antonio Canova and Bertel Thorvaldson. History paintings, a common Neoclassical genre, served as visual allegories that taught lessons on heroism and moral virtue. Neoclassical figurative painting, sculpture, and architectural programs depicted the deeds of great and powerful men, formally and thematically. By reviving Classical Roman figurative forms particularly, Neoclassical artists sought to portray eternal beauty and cultural idealism, embodied often in balanced, symmetrical, and "able," or extra-able bodies. Therefore, Neoclassicism, and the Classical heritage it adopts, communicates social and political ideals through aesthetics. In Western culture from the Renaissance to the present day, this form is characteristically employed for public statues of idealized religious and political heroes.

Quinn subverts the signification of the Neoclassical "ideal" in *Alison Lapper Pregnant* and his many life-size marble sculptures of amputees, in the series *The Complete Marbles* (2002). With these works, he challenges how the viewer judges the body in art, as well as in everyday life as whole and/or amputated. The sculptures resemble Classical and Neoclassical statuary, and are titled with the proper names of their subjects. Quinn's sculptural depiction of amputee historical subjects, among them the artist and friend of Lapper's, Peter Hull, adopts Neoclassical qualities of portrait and history painting, as well as the characteristics of Roman sculpture to depict portrait likeness. The works confuse perceptions of figurative art as symbolic and/or specific to the portrait subject. Quinn's use of some high profile disabled models, such as the confrontational "freak" performer and punk rock musician, Matt Fraser, makes the works recognizable as depictions of celebrities. The display of the body as public art, in *Alison Lapper Pregnant*, heightens the tendencies to see the body as purely symbolic or allegorical, another quotation of Neoclassical conventions. Public statues portray social values through subjects who become representative of particular historical events or political movements. Significantly, these subjects are most often men, whose public personas and images are recognizable. In contrast, women's bodies as public statuary are most often allegorical and serve as decorative objects. Art historical representation of the body as symbolic allegory in is a trope that Marina Warner (1985) has associated with women's bodies in particular, as images of "Woman" that are constructed by men.[9] The statue of Alison Lapper oscillates between these traditions. The fact that the sculpture is three times the size of Lapper herself, who is only 3 feet and 1 inch tall, inflates her presence visually and symbolically, taking her beyond the realm of everyday. The nature of the carved, smooth marble heightens the somewhat disembodied, ethereal qualities of the work;[10] however Lapper's unique corporeality, the discourse surrounding the work, and Lapper's specific life story breach boundaries between the personal (individual) and public (symbolic).

Quinn's works invoke the body as allegory, as well as monument, strategically. One the few works in *The Complete Marbles* that is not titled with the models' names, *Kiss* (2002), refers to a specific canonical sculpture in art history, Auguste Rodin's *The Kiss* (1886). Quinn's *Kiss* features two life-size amputees cast from live models (Matt Fraser and artist Catherine Long), leaning against one another (rather than seated, as in Rodin's original), to embrace passionately. Fraser's shortened arms caress Long's left shoulder and armless "stump." Quinn here showcases disabled lovers as contemporary social subjects, in an animated portrait or symbol of romantic love, and as sexual beings, showing a different side of amputees than the viewer may be used to seeing in contexts of art history and popular culture. The amputees here serve as an allegory of love; simultaneously, they represent a love story with specific political connotations, as the amorous pose challenges stereotypes of disability as sexually undesirable. *Kiss* and other works in *The Complete Marbles* series are portraits that call for revisions of art history and social ideals, particularly by merging perceptions of the body as allegory and as portrait subject simultaneously.

Quinn's riding of the fence in this way appears too ambivalent for some. Many have seen Quinn's framing of the amputee body as critically subversive, specifically of Neoclassicism. For example, art writer for the *Sunday Times* Waldemar Januszczak (2000) states the following about *Allison Lapper Pregnant*:

> By carving Allison Lapper out of pristine marble, Quinn is *taking on* the Greeks; he is *disputing* with Phidias, with Michelangelo, with Sir Joshua Reynolds, with every authoritarian with imagination that has ever insisted upon a standard shape for the human in art; he is contradicting 2,000 years of creative *misrepresentation* of what being human means; and he is giving Allison Lapper the same amount of artistic attention that Canova gave the Empress Josephine. As if that were not enough, Quinn is also cheekily rhyming his sculptures with the broken remnants of classical art—the armless Venus, the legless Apollo—that are the staple diet of all collections of the antique. These are serious achievements.[11] (Emphasis mine)

My italics here underscore how Januszczak describes Quinn's use of amputees in art historical, specifically Classical and Neoclassical images, as confrontational and revisionist, as if the works are affronts to these traditions because of the amputees featured. This comment suggests that certain social prejudices against amputees function in critical interpretations of Quinn's work. Quinn's works are indeed confrontational, as they force viewers to question their immediate associations and judgments of bodies, amputees specifically. Yet, they are not nearly as assaulting as Januszczak implies to the viewer and to art historical conventions.

A relevant, highly confrontational counterexample, a photograph by Joel-Peter Witkin, *Canova's Venus, New York City* (1982), puts Quinn's engagement with Neoclassicism into perspective. Januszczak points to particular canonical sculptures by Neoclassical artist Antonio Canova, who was a favorite painter of Napoleon Bonaparte and produced numerous Neoclassical likenesses of the Bonaparte family. The work referenced by Januszczak is akin to the work Witkin parodies: a famous sculpture of Napoleon's sister, *Paolina Borghese as Venus Victrix* (1808) (also called *Pauline Bonaparte*), an allegorical portrait of a historical subject in the guise of a Venus, particularly the *Victrix*, meaning "victorious" or "the conqueress." Canova's sculpture blends the Classical traditions of displaying the eroticized female body as an allegorical seductress, combined with the portrait likeness of a specific aristocratic individual, in idealizing Neoclassical form. The work's title refers to the Judgment of Paris, a Classical myth in which the goddess Venus wins a beauty contest and therefore receives an apple from Paris (included in Paolina's hand), and this event also became the mythical beginning of the bloody Trojan War and the inspiration for canonical Greek epics. The myth depicted and embodied in Canova's Neoclassical rendering of Paolina suggests the ambivalent status of women and women's bodies, their control over the earth and heavens, and their potential power over the actions of men in Classical mythology, as well as in the highly patriarchal Neoclassical movements. This ambivalence becomes the target of Witkin's subversive quotation.

Witkin's black and white photographic version, *Canova's Venus, New York City* (1982), shines a huge spotlight on the inherent contradictions of Neoclassical and other idealizing forms, emphasized by the graphic medium of photography. The photograph stages an androgynous, preoperative transsexual model holding an apple, signifying the Judgment of Paris, as well as Biblical themes of man's fall from in grace and man's degradation in the face of a Christian God, specifically by the seductions and knowledge of women. Witkin's Venus is anatomically male, yet sexually ambiguous and decidedly feminized in his aquiline profile (again, a clinical convention), which outlines feminine, chiseled (sculptural) features and

delicate, small hands. Male pectorals with erect nipples (one emphasized in profile), surrounded by subtle chest hair, displays the body as
aroused, erotic, and feminized in the act of sexual display. The pose
of the model is twisted in comparison with the original to display his
corporeality for the camera. A "treasure trail" leads the eyes to the
exposed genitals and pubic hair, details that make this Neoclassical
nude pornographically naked. The drapery fails to conceal the body,
and rather showcases the penis; in a literal and figurative twist on
the Classical and Neoclassical traditions, the drapery functions
simultaneously to visually articulate and display the sexualized
body. Witkin's Venus images, such as this one, call attention to the
exploitation of all bodies in art history. His works target specifically
the artistic conventions that make such displays aesthetically justifi-
able. Here, the drapery is significantly stained with ink splotches, as
Witkin literally and photographically tarnishes or contaminates art
historical conventions for representing the nude.

In comparison, Quinn's subversion of Classical and Neoclassical
ideals is far more subtle. Witkin's Neoclassical drag show exaggerates the spectacle nature of Canova's original display in heightened
sensationalism and pornographic overtones, versus the subdued
elegance of Quinn's work. Quinn's works lose the Classical draper-
ies, as if to remove the element of deception or representational
artifice. Rather than corrupting Neoclassicism with "damaged"
amputees, as some critics have assumed, Quinn uses these culturally
familiar forms, and the beauty ideals associated with them, as
contexts in which to display amputees. Quinn's sculptures aim to
carve out new, progressive images of disability, and with his acknow-
ledged intention.

Quinn titled his series of marble amputees *The Complete Marbles*
also strategically. Particularly in a British context, this title references
stolen masterpieces taken out of the original context for public display. *The Elgin Marbles* are precious Classical sculptures appropri-
ated from the Parthenon in Greece (produced c. 438–423 BCE) and
exhibited in the British Museum for the past 150 years. They have
continuously been the source of dispute between the British and
Greek governments on ownership rights. These works were "stolen,"
not in terms of theoretical, deconstructive appropriation, but rather
for their cultural desirability and material value. *The Elgin Marbles*
are broken off from their architectural base (the Parthenon) and

are fragments of profoundly aesthetic "wholes," for the Parthenon remains remarkable today for its integrated, carefully orchestrated balance and proportion and intense, methodical control of aesthetics. Its status as a cultural icon is tied to aesthetic "wholeness." Extracted from the Temple to Athena, the goddess of wisdom, the marbles both fragment and represent one of the greatest symbols of power and wealth in Western history. Quinn's title for the series, *The Complete Marbles*, places contemporary disabled bodies in these historical legacies, and they are designated as "whole" by their own counter-conventional body standards.

The title of the series points to their corporeal and subjective "wholeness;" they are indeed, "complete." Within the vernacular phrasing that someone has "lost their marbles," the sculptures' designation as "complete" implies a state of wisdom, peace of mind, and rationality—again, a reference spiraling back to notions of the ideal body as rationally or mathematically, and therefore ideally coherent, in Classical and Neoclassical philosophy and embodied in figurative sculpture. Quinn's studies of art history at Cambridge inform much of his work, and he acknowledges this influence (and one he shares with Witkin), yet says he is more interested in how art history frames perception, rather than corrupting or deconstructing the discipline itself. In regard to the amputee sculptures, Quinn expresses interest in how seeing something in marble differs from seeing it in the flesh, and why some find one form over another distasteful or shocking.[12] However, many find Quinn's ambivalence disturbing, or at least discomforting, and demand more "complete" explanation on his intentions by displaying disability, particularly within traditionally idealizing forms.

### Heroes and Spectacles

The formal qualities of *Alison Lapper Pregnant* have been the target of much criticism; however, criticisms against the artistic value of *Alison Lapper Pregnant* (the work) may suggest simultaneous rejection of Alison Lapper pregnant (as an embodiment and social subject). For example, art critic David Lee summed up his opinion of the sculpture as "ghastly."[13] Many critics have charged Quinn with capitalizing on the shock value[14] of disabled bodies in public spaces, implying that disability is somehow inherently shocking and taboo, rather than quite integral to notions of the "public" itself and to universal humanity. The work makes these stereotypes visible. Jonathan Jones of the *Guardian* has called the work "bad art" and argues that the human interest story of Alison Lapper eclipses any consideration of its aesthetic value. For Jones and others, Lapper's story evokes the cliché that disabled people deserve pity, which makes them special cases and therefore critically untouchable "others."[15] These attitudes are based on low expectations of what disabled people can do to the effect that people with impairments who perform even mundane tasks of everyday life are deemed "heroes," condescendingly.

Positive evaluations of the *Alison Lapper Pregnant* complicate how the sculpture represents disability in the public eye, as they purport Lapper to be a hero. In support of the work, London Mayor Ken Livingstone stated "*Alison Lapper Pregnant* is a modern heroine—strong, formidable and full of hope."[16] This comment recalls the stereotype of a disabled hero that is based in sentimental- ization and assumed weaknesses of disabled people in society. What kind of hero is Lapper in these descriptions, one who dismantles notions of appropriate versus shocking bodies, or one who rehashes the stereotype of "overcoming," which ignores social constructs of disability and reaffirms the notion of disability as an individual "problem" of an individual body? Framed as the representation of a heroine, the sculpture celebrates Lapper's impairments and perhaps also depoliticizes, or literally aestheticizes disability, as a restric- tive social construct, for the public. Or perhaps it redefines our ideas about heroism and makes a disabled figure a role model, in a positive light.

Lapper's heroism may also be problematically tied to her preg- nancy, such that motherhood becomes a means for Lapper to "overcome" disability by conforming to standards for women's roles in society, a point that Kim Q. Hall (2006) has interrogated.[17] Hall quotes Quinn's own words about the work: "For me, *Alison Lapper Pregnant* is a monument to the future possibilities of the human race as well as the resilience of the human spirit."[18] Hall frames this com- ment within political propaganda that has imposed the duty upon women historically to reproduce the nation; such dogma is simi- lar to that expressed throughout Trafalgar Square by the national heroes depicted. Hall argues that the sculpture is championed by Quinn and many others because it conforms to mainstream, patriarchal, and heterosexual values. Yet, Hall's persuasive arguments reframe how Lapper's presence in the Square plays upon traditional gender roles and disability stereotypes only tangentially, for the sculpture's and Lapper's own consistent divergence from convention affirms its adamant nonconformity to "family values." Far from glorifying a nuclear family, Lapper was born to a single, working-class mother and is herself an unmarried mother, who has lived off public assistance for disabled people and public programs for disabled artists. She hardly acts in the legacy of national heroes. Nationalistic and mainstream discourses that breed women for motherhood suggest that a productive female member of the society is a *reproductive* one, specifically within the institution of marriage. Many may view Lapper's choices amoral and her subsistence as a public burden. Further, the increasing devaluation of the arts in a big business and science-oriented society raises questions about the role of artists as productive citizens, let alone single mothers with disabilities.

Lapper's maternal situation defies ideals of both society and art for women's bodies. Pregnant bodies, seen most often in art history as fertility figures, occupy a liminal status, as both an ideal state of the female motherhood, yet one that contrasts with the conventions for the sexualized nude. Fertility figures in Western and non-Western cultures feature robust forms that are conceived as "fat" by today's standards; although more popular representations have tended to idealize pregnancy socially, they also veil the pregnant female body, reinstating its preferred existence within the proverbial home. Images of pregnant women are becoming trendy lately, particularly among the elite, with the celebrity "baby boom" displayed in the aesthetic "bumps" on otherwise perfect bodies and within the romanticized unions of the Brangelinas and Tom-Kats of the world; Demi Moore, Melania Trump, Katie Holmes, and Britney Spears have been featured in mainstream women's magazines as so-called liberated cover girls and centerfolds, revealing their scantily clad, eroticized, and fashionable pregnant bodies. Again, these pregnant bodies are framed specifically within dominant social ideals and values, to which Alison Lapper could never conform. *Alison Lapper Pregnant* confuses perceptions of images of the body in art history and popular culture, ultimately because, for many, the work assertively provokes the fear that the disabled body will reproduce another "damaged" child—from a "broken" body and a "broken" home. The work in this way advocates potentially controversial reproductive rights for disabled women and for single women more broadly. Further, any attempt on Lapper's part to fulfill her role to reproduce the next generation may produce a disabled one, which remains a horror rather than a triumph, according to mainstream values and exclusive social standards for beauty, health, individual duty, and the quality of life. Lapper's maternal "acts" poignantly fail to service such ideals, as the sculpture becomes pregnant with ambivalent meaning, metaphorically and literally.

Quinn has engaged with themes of birth and other biological/sociological human processes across his oeuvres, and his past use of graphic bodily materials influences the charge that his works capitalize on shock value. Quinn has a certain reputation as a "bad boy" among art critics, a precedence set by the inclusion of his work in the controversial *Sensation* exhibit of 1991. In this exhibit, most famously lambasted by the New York Major Rudy Giuliani, when it traveled to the United States, Quinn debuted one of his most famous pieces, *Self* (1991), a self-portrait bust made from 9 pints of Quinn's frozen and preserved blood. Some have connected *Alison Lapper Pregnant* with a longer interest in birth in Quinn's work, as exemplified by *Birth* or *Lucas* (2001), a frozen representation of his son Lucas's head made from real three day old placenta. His work has many such bodily and biological themes; Quinn has worked with DNA imaging (*DNA Garden* (2002), a grid of 77 Petri dishes), test tubes, and silicon preservation. Additional examples of Quinn's work with body fluids and forms are: *Yellow Cut Nervous Breakdown, Invisible Man, No Invisible Means of Escape XI* (formed from cast white rubber resembling flesh), *The Great Escape* (a cast of his body inside a pod), *Continuous Present* (2000) (featuring a skull that rotates around a reflective cylinder), *Shit Paintings* and *Shit Head* (1997), *Incarnate* (a boiled sausage formed again from his blood), *Eternal Spring* I and II (1998) (a series featuring Calla lilies suspended in water), and *Garden* (2000) (a glass walled installation of flora and fauna that was deceptively composed of frozen units of silicon). As exemplified by these pieces, Quinn's work has repeatedly used blood, placenta, excrement, ice, and flowers. Quinn chooses these bodily substances, reminiscent of still life elements (in use of heads, skulls, and flowers, for examples) because of their corporeality and symbolic connotations, which surpass art historical iconography. These materials represent for Quinn larger interests in self/other social dynamics, for they are often associated with abjection, the materiality of body, and vulnerability of the flesh.[19] Art writer Mark Gisbourne (2002) states that *Self* and Quinn's other works in this vein are concerned with what constitutes acceptance, desire/repulsion, and rejection of body forms and processes, and that these themes continue in his marble amputees.[20]

Quinn's oeuvre in bodily fluids and other biological materials presents a questionable context for his work with amputees. Embodying themes of mortality, duality, birth, and sexuality, Quinn's previous works may present frameworks that medicalize and sensationalize the subjects of *The Complete Marbles* and *Alison Lapper Pregnant*. The works described above portray themes of artistic and scientific displays graphically and many have been included in thematic exhibitions of works that engage historical medical imagery and explore histories of medical spectacles.[21] *Self*, for example, is reminiscent of body parts kept preserved in fluids, a form characteristic of medical displays, as well as the preservation of Christian saints' blood in reliquaries. Such materials also reference fluids preserved for medical use in practices such as transfusions and organ replacement—surgical procedures in which body parts enter into and merge with other bodies. In addition, Quinn's reference to Neoclassicism places all of his amputee statues in a historical context populated by physiognomic discourses and representations. Physiognomy purported that inner character was displayed on the body and in physical features. Nineteenth-century scientists and artists invoked these ideals through visual renderings of the body to express emotion, character, and supposedly fixed and biologically determined personality characteristics. Measurements and visualizations of morality and character following physiognomic principles focused particularly on corporeal indications of pathology and deviance. Physiognomic displays paralleled anatomical exhibits in making the body, particularly the abnormal body, into a spectacle. Quinn's sculptures, while quoting artistic forms, evoke also histories of medical displays of amputees and other so-called pathological bodies, which were often life-sized and made from wax. The use of wax made such figures eerily lifelike, despite that often their insides, also rendered in wax, were the main attraction. Pregnant women, particularly revealing the fetus inside, were popular subjects for anatomical wax models, a visual history that may taint the display of *Alison Lapper Pregnant* by associating the work with medical models and spectacles, visually and thematically.

Indeed, Lapper's unique medical history, chronicled in her memoir as a series of objectifying and shameful displays of her body by doctors to "instruct" their peers on deformity and anomaly, connects intimately in the process of the work's production. Lapper describes in detail the laborious process of being cast by Quinn and his assistants in plaster, a material that crosses art and medical use. She notes that having multiple eyes and hands on her nude body, covering it in a cocoon-like, smothering and sticky shroud, was not that shocking for her, because of her many childhood medical exams and surgeries, as well as the casting of her body for her own self-portrait work.[22] Yet Quinn's 2000 work of Lapper with her 5-month-old son, Parys, on her lap contrasts glaringly with medical models that rip open the female body for display of anatomy. The marble in particular places this work in a history of reverent sculptures of the Madonna and infant Jesus. Such deeply historical and religious images of pathos contrast strikingly with medical context for displaying "pathology."

Quinn's procedures and uses of materials are central to the significances of all of his works. His seemingly seamless craftsmanship in marble diverges from wax and other medical models attempts to depict the flesh. Like all of the pieces in *The Complete Marbles*, *Alison Lapper Pregnant* was cast in Quinn's studio, made into a macquette that was taken to Pietrasenta, Italy, the center for work with Carrara marble—the same marble sought by Michelangelo. *Alison Lapper Pregnant* took 10 months to craft from the substance, which is hard and stubborn and embodies exalted histories and symbolic significances. Quinn is quite particular about the material, as he literally goes out of his way to use it, and he prefers this marble, like his choices of biological materials in his other works, for its "intrinsic and metaphoric content."[23] Carrara marble provides a luminosity that makes his amputees shine and radiate, likening the works to sculptures from the later Greek Hellenistic era (marked by the death of Alexander in 326 BCE and continuing to the Roman period of the first century CE), to which lustrous and glittering surface treatments were often applied. Also relevant to *The Complete Marbles*, Hellenistic works exhibited a shift in Classical Greek sculpture from the depiction of gods to the portrayal of mortals, in poses that best conveyed the drama of human emotion. The subjects of *The Complete Marbles* strike predominantly active, dynamic postures; they sit with shortened or amputated arms extended, balance on one leg to perform a martial arts sidekick (ironically, with a thigh-length leg), stand at attention, embrace while standing on one leg, and repose classically with one leg bended. Many of these poses are visually similar to the humanistic, expressionistic figures of the Hellenistic period, which performatively interacted with the viewer, in solicitations of identification and empathy. The poses of *The Complete Marbles* refer also to the Elgin Marbles' portrayal of Greek myths and battles in graceful, powerful movements. Further, *The Complete Marbles*, by invoking *The Elgin Marbles,* refer to scenes of pilgrimage to the shrine of Athena that are images of worship, as well as of mobility. These works embody multiple associations, while refusing to diagnose the subjects' impairments and therefore distorting the rational, scientific content of Neoclassical figures and pseudoscientific themes of physiognomy. The fine marble crafting brings to the amputee portraits specific art historical traditions, ones that grant them the status of precious and revered objects. The work embodies, but also transgresses classifications of disabled people as heroes and freaks.

## Public Demonstrations

Such dubious, or perhaps simply overwhelming contexts for viewing the body, as well as Quinn's notorious reputation, conflate in the responses to *Alison Lapper Pregnant*. Many viewers desire more straightforward answers about the work's message. Notions that the work is shocking and/or inspiring seem polarized, and yet both connote, to varying degrees, the desire to make a lesson out of the disabled body, in order to justify its display. Many who critique this work and Quinn's *Complete Marbles* demand explanation about the cause of disability and its usefulness to nondisabled people. For example, *Sunday Times* writer Waldemar Januszczak (2000) states, "With a subject as serious as the loss of human limbs, or the birth of a child to a deformed mother, it is absolutely incumbent upon the gallery to cease playing aesthetic games and to make clearer the artist's intentions."[24] Such a call for additional commentary expresses a need for medical diagnosis to make the works more palatable and less sensationalistic. However, the sculpture also provokes some viewers to question their own desires to "know," and to question the assumption that the disabled body connotes victimization or a medical mistake. In a letter to the editor, Hanne Olsen stated, "Disabled bodies are only accepted when attached to a 'worthy message.' *Alison Lapper Pregnant* is one of the few examples in the public domain of disability portrayed in an assertive and uncompromising composition and does much to counteract the usual depiction of disabled people as victims."[25] Olson refers to the problematic use of the disabled body pervasively in literature and visual representation, as expounded upon by disability studies theorists Mitchell and Snyder (2000) as symbolic of something other than human embodiment, most often tragedy, disaster, or chaos and psychic instability. Mitchell and Snyder argue that the narrative serves often as a "prosthesis" to disability, thus functioning at the site of impairment. The overwhelming view of disability as pitiful and shameful is overturned in Lapper's bold self-exhibition and constructed heroism. The work therefore forges important public dialogues about disability and resists one-dimensional readings, for Olsen and many others.

Olsen's views address complicated issues surrounding the use of any body as a monument. The canonical history painting preferred during Neoclassical times depicted the Classical body in compositions meant to teach moral lessons through idealistic and heroic depiction of historical events. The figures served in historical and moral instruction, and the adherence to Neoclassical conventions for public statuary continues this tradition. Further, the notion that the disabled body must present a social lesson is relevant to the realm of public art and for monuments specifically. Public art in general, in the tradition of monuments, has a duty, in the eyes of many, to educate and inform. The origin of the word "monument" "derives from Latin *nomere,* meaning "to remind," "to admonish," "warn," "advise," and "instruct."[26] Monuments remind and instruct the public about historical events and people through visual mediation. Poignantly, this word origin emerges also in the word "monster," as scholars of the freak show have pointed out to explain how the disabled body has historically been seen as monstrous and therefore indicating either supernatural foreshadowing or scientific mistake. The use of the disabled body for scientific instruction has included public exploitation of so-called medical anomalies, practices which have reinforced medical models and crossed genres into freak shows.

The freak show is a relevant comparison for considering the role of Lapper's disabled body in a public space, particularly one that serves as a tourist attraction and is already populated with nationalistic British monuments, which I will discuss in detail below. The nineteenth- and early-twentieth-century freak show staged the disabled body as a spectacle to affirm the opposing normality of the middle class spectator. It depended on the shock value of disability, as does the attraction of *Alison Lapper Pregnant*, as many have argued. "She is presented like some 19th-century fairground exhibit," one critic stated.[27] The statue is monumental in size and elevated on a pedestal, which separates it off from the everyday viewer, just as the disabled freak was specifically staged as a distanced and extraordinary "other." The freak show characteristically eroticized the disabled and other extraordinary (exotic, minority) bodies for the draw of voyeurs, similarly to pornography, an industry that also blossomed during this time period. *Alison Lapper Pregnant* may be considered pornographic for some viewers who are shocked by its state of undress. The nudity of the sculpture is intrinsic to its unashamed display of the pregnant, disabled body and to its Neoclassical form, for nudity places the work in a both a history of art and a history of displaying the body as spectacle, in the freak show, pornography and other voyeuristic venues. Finally, the freak body was exploited and commodified for the profit of the showman, and indeed, following its limited appearance on the fourth plinth, *Alison Lapper Pregnant* is up for sale for 500,000 pounds. These factors underscore a weighty question: does the sculpture exploit Alison Lapper?

I don't wish to dwell here on whether or not Alison Lapper was compensated monetarily for her modeling, for she has repeatedly affirmed her decision to pose nude for Quinn and is benefiting from the attention the work has drawn to her own art and her life, as she published a memoir (2005). The story of her life underscores the tremendous personal and political weight of her participation in the public sculpture of her body, for she grew up in isolated homes for children, with limited engagement with larger society. She laments how her sexuality was repressed and discouraged in the institutions specifically. Public exposure, for Lapper, surpasses that fact that she is nude in the work and displayed as sexually active. In the memoir, she relates *Alison Lapper Pregnant* to her own self-portrait nude photography, with which she expresses comfort in her own skin and challenges her personal history of being considered physically defective and sexually unattractive. Addressing the controversy regarding the nudity of the statue, Lapper has written, "In most societies, even in Britain today, pregnant women are not considered to have a beautiful shape. On top of that, short people, who are missing both arms, are generally considered even less beautiful. I was someone who currently combined both disadvantages. How could Marc possibly think I was a suitable subject for a sculpture that people would want to look at? Statues are created and exhibited to give pleasure, to be admired. Would anybody be able to admire the statue of a naked, pregnant, disabled woman?"[28] She attributes the controversy of the sculpture to a society that is prudish to nudity in general, as well as to pregnancy and disability specifically. Many may deem the work amoral, and therefore in direct opposition to Neoclassical, moralistic traditions, and yet, as Lapper articulates, moral judgments are subjective to the eyes of the beholders.

Lapper does not express feeling exploited. Describing her decision to pose, Lapper writes in her memoir: "It was January 1999 when I received a phone call from an artist called Marc Quinn. . . . I was extremely suspicious. I thought he might be just another one in the long line of people who have exploited disability and used it for its curiosity and value. However, when we talked, I realised Marc wasn't interested in disability in the way most people wanted to depict it. He wasn't pitying or moralising—I knew it wasn't a freak show or some kind of weird sexual focus that he was aiming at."[29] Lapper here recognizes the problematic tropes of representing disabled bodies as sentimentalized heroes or freakish spectacles, both of which make the disabled body into a symbol and lesson to the learned by the so-called normal. Poignantly, she ties these tropes together. The work functions to make stereotypes visible and part of public debate, in which Lapper herself participates. Further, by collaborating with Quinn, Lapper makes a statement about the need for public education and exposure of/to disability as a multidimensional experience in order to overturn the stereotypes and the status quo.

## Trafalgar Square Unveiled

Trafalgar Square is an ideal place to raise and interrogate such issues of bodily representation. The modern city, and public squares like Trafalgar especially, were built for tourist gazing, urban surveillance, and commercial spectatorship.[30] Historian Rodney Mace (1976) chronicles how urban initiatives, such as the building of Trafalgar Square, transformed the social landscape through a widening and "cleansing" of streets, pushed the lower classes to the margins, closed down local traders and vendors, and offered social interactions centered on big business.[31] Trafalgar Square, designed by John Nash and built by Sir Charles Barry in the 1820s and 1830s to commemorate British naval captain and famous imperialist Admiral Horatio Nelson (1758–1805), was named after the Spanish Cape Trafalgar where Nelson's last battle was won. Characteristic of this period's revival of Roman Classicism in Britain, the Square's architecture and statuary is specifically Neoclassical to portray political ideals. A monument to Lord Nelson became the central vision of the Square in the 1840s and still dominates the scene. A Neoclassical likeness of Nelson stands on a 185 foot tall column, overseeing or overshadowing the diverse general public, a legacy that continues today. At the base of the columns are reliefs, titled "Copenhagen," "The Nile," "St. Vincent," and "Trafalgar," that depict scenes of Nelson's moments in famous battles (from the late 1700s to early 1800s), as well as large, imposing protective lion statues. Nelson's monument was modeled after the triumphant, politically propagandistic Roman Column of Trajan (named for Roman emperor Trajan and erected in 113–116 or after 117 CE). This Roman precedence continues throughout the Neoclassical architecture of the Square, placing modern Britain in the traditions of Roman imperialism. Surrounding Nelson are other monuments to British military "heroes" (i.e., imperialists), represented in idealizing and exonerating forms. At the south end of the square is an equestrian statue of Charles I in a conventional pose suggesting royalty and conquest, which is based on a famous

Roman statue of Marcus Aurelius and was also the favored position of Louis XV and Napoleon to emphasize their military strength and leadership (for example in David's triumphant, Neoclassical portrait *Napoleon Crossing the Alps* (1801), which served as Imperial propaganda). On both sides of Nelson's Column are the bronze statues of Sir Henry Havelock and Sir Charles James Napier, and fronting the north wall of Trafalgar are busts of Generals Beatty, Jellicoe, and Cunningham, all famous military leaders. All of the "heroes" who populate the square are significantly honored for their participation in the colonization of India, Egypt, and the Caribbean, and were known in their times as brutal leaders of mutinous soldiers, who were often of the nationality of the countries they fought to dominate. Many of the military men commemorated side by side in Trafalgar Square also feuded with one another. Like the design of the square, the monuments display a particular side of British history and society, one whose power depends on the subordination of those rendered invisible. Erected in Neoclassical forms, these men's bodies serve as landmarks of patriarchal and colonist British histories.

With its marble, feminine curves and serene posture, *Alison Lapper Pregnant* would seem out of place in such a paternalistic environment[32]—the antihero. And yet others see the sculpture as right at home with the other monuments. Lapper has been compared symbolically and corporeally with Admiral Nelson himself; for example, in a letter to the editor, Michael Gallagher calls Lapper "[a] great Briton in the truest sense of the word. I am sure that Nelson would have recognised her as a kindred spirit," and Jeanette Hart, from Lewisham in London, notes (2005), "Nelson only had one arm, and was blind in one eye, and he was just known as a great man; no one labelled him."[33] Nelson was indeed blinded in one eye during the capture of Corsica from French troops in 1794, lost his arm in a 1797 invasion of the Canary Islands, and continued to lead troops with these impairments until his death at the Battle of Trafalgar in 1805, an act which has augmented his status as a national hero. Nelson's Column is topped by a statue of Nelson poised with his uniform coat sleeve draped along his chest and tucked into his suit, in a conventional pose for leaders, yet his sleeve is empty. However, this "lack" is not perceptible for the viewer below, due to the height of the column, as the structure veils and symbolically mediates his corporeal impairments.

Nonetheless, Quinn's public display of Alison Lapper has illuminated for some viewers, such as Hart, that the disabled body is always already present in and part of an existing vision of heroism, as the work reinterprets notions of disabled and nondisabled heroes. Framing Lapper as a hero reinterprets or expands the image of a heroic body, and perhaps her designation as a hero does not simply rehash stereotypes, but rather describes the meaning of her body as a public image within a specific location and historical context. In her memoir, Lapper reflects on others seeing her as a hero and expresses flattery rather than indignation. The fourth plinth she now occupies has remained vacant from the opening of the square until 1990, due to ongoing financial constraints, and perhaps her heroic presence is not a break with tradition, but quite appropriate and even long overdue.

By occupying the status of both hero and antihero, monument and antimonument, Lapper follows in multiple histories of public art that are celebratory of or in protest to their context, the latter of which tends to characterize contemporary or new genre public art. All of the submissions for the Fourth Plinth project competition since 1990 have been consciously critical of the square's aristocratic, nationalistic, and paternalistic traditions, both in content and form. As art critic Paul Usherwood (2004) describes it, Lapper carries on this contemporary trend of mocking the square's "macho triumphalism and formality."[34] Lapper's Neo- or post-Classical form embodies also a breaching of boundaries between convention and subversion. And by embodying contradictions, Lapper once again fits right into Trafalgar Square and translates its history to contemporary debates over civil and human rights. The controversial debates surrounding the work continue a long-standing history of Trafalgar Square, which has been wrought with conflict historically (as evidenced by the background stories on the lives of the men honored there). Trafalgar Square has served as the city's most popular rallying point and the site of political, economic, and religious protests; interventions of military law; class battles; protests for freedom of speech and rights to assemble, for women's suffrage, and for civil rights, liberties, and decolonization; and pro and antiwar, pro and anti-Fascism and Semitism, and pro and anticommunism rallies.[35] Poignantly, all these displays of activism represent multiple and opposing sides of social and political issues since the nineteenth century and, significantly, most of these demonstrations have centered on the base of Nelson's column, because of its physical prominence and its symbolic significance. Nelson again proves to bear connections with Lapper's body on display, for both embody multiple significances contextually and historically and have been witnesses to multiplicities of perspectives. Both Nelson's and Lapper's bodies in Trafalgar Square pay tribute to the necessity of public debate.

The sculpture of Alison Lapper and its social and symbolic meanings must be considered within its specific context. The work embodies, transforms, and contemporizes the history of its space. Characteristic of public work that makes social and political impact, *Alison Lapper Pregnant* forges change, enacts rupture, and is as dynamic and dialectic as the "public" itself, even, or perhaps especially, in her serene pose.[36] Trafalgar Square has served historically as site of many struggles between government and people about their social relationships and the dynamics of power. It symbolizes both long-standing and contemporary political platforms, dissents, and dialogues about the control of ideas and expressions. The sculpture of Lapper carries on these traditions of debate and dissent by provoking discussion. The controversy and many opposing opinions expressed publicly about the sculpture enact its social work. Art historian Patricia Phillips (1992) writes, "Public art has been too often applied as a modest antidote or a grand solution, rather than perceived as a forum for investigation, articulation, and constructive appraisal. Although it is an exploratory stage, public art is treated as if it were a production of fixed strategies and principles."[37] Phillips advocates for public art that resists closure, provokes change, and indeed, gives birth to debate.

Lapper's "expecting" body on display has provoked constructive investigation about the role of art in society and the roles of disabled bodies as heroes and spectacles. It asks us to interrogate our definitions of hero and our assumptions about what forms of bodies should or should not appear in public spaces and how. The dubious representations of disability the work evokes are both liberating and stereotypical, which is necessary to provoke discussion. Like all performances, the work itself is temporary, which Phillips also advocates is necessary for public art to be dialectical. Yet the discussions it raises will hopefully continue beyond the piece and beyond the body of Lapper. Many have begun to express the same hope and, poignantly, have come to understand disability as a social construction and to question their perceptions, as articulated in an editorial by Andrew Crooks (2004): "The sculpture has also uncovered the attitudes of society that pregnant disabled women are shocking. What actually seems shocking are the negative and damaging attitudes it provokes.[38] Such countercriticism and public examination and exposure are what the sculpture demands. That Lapper herself has been so vocal in the discussions is key, for her collaboration with Quinn and her public mediation of the work show how perspectives of disability, not just about them, are necessary for any productive dialogue.

### Presenting Alison Lapper

Dialogues between Quinn's work and Lapper's own body art, which self-narrates her experiences as a disabled woman artist, provide significant discussions about disability and visual representation. Lapper was born in 1965 to single, working-class mother, with no upper limbs and foreshortened lower limbs. The hospital predicted a grim, and likely short future, yet Lapper proved to be a survivor. Her mother chose not to try to raise her, so Lapper lived and attended school at Chailey Heritage School in East Sussex from six weeks to seventeen years old, and then went to a disability assessment centre of the Queen Elizabeth's Foundation for Disabled People at Banstead in Surrey, where she learned skills for living independently and enrolled in the Sutton College of Learning for Adults to pursue an art degree. Lapper remembers art as her favorite and most successful class, particularly in comparison with other subjects, for she had undiagnosed and therefore unaccommodated dyslexia. She also remarks on having to prove herself repeatedly to nondisabled people, intellectually, artistically, personally, and sexually, due to assumptions about her so-called lacking anatomy. She moved to London at age nineteen, where she lived independently for the first time, and she later attended the University of Brighton, graduated with a degree in fine art at age twenty-eight, purchased a home in Southwick, and continues to work as an artist. Lapper has been the focus of the BBC One series *Child of Our Time* program, to which she has returned for annual appearances, and an hour long documentary by Milton Media for Denmark's TV2, titled *Alison's Baby*, which has been broadcast in many countries and won the Prix Italia and the Prix Leonardo. In 2003, Lapper won the MBE (Member of the British Empire) award for service to the arts. Since graduation from Brighton, she has worked fulltime for the Mouth and Foot Painting Artists' Association of England (MFPA). Funding for this program comes from the artists' production of decorative images for cards designs, marketed by the MFPA, and Lapper writes that she still enjoys producing such genre scenes and landscapes, along with her self-portrait work.

Lapper's self-portrait body art, in the forms of photography, sculpture, and installation, began as and continues to be part of a process of self-discovery. At the University of Brighton, an opinionated viewer challenged the nature of Lapper's figurative work of nondisabled bodies, as was the common practice in her art school, by suggesting that perhaps Lapper had not fully accepted her own body. This moment became a turning point for Lapper, as she began envisioning her own body as a work of art. Her inspiration for this "coming out" was a photograph of the Venus de Milo, in which she saw her own likeness. Lapper began casting her body in plaster sculptures (with the help of friends) at the University of Brighton and then photographing herself in Venus-like poses, as she took on the Venus de Milo as her body image. Her graduation exhibit featured an installation the viewer had to enter on hands and knees, at the height level of Lapper herself, in order to see photographs and sculpted casts of her full body and body parts. This installation created an environment that removed the viewer from their own comfort zone physically and perceptively and explored the relationships between the viewer's and Lapper's acts of looking at, judging, and experiencing her body.

Her self-portrait work and her personifications specifically of the Venus de Milo, like Duffy's, explore the complicated interactions of disability and sexuality, particularly for women. Lapper's shameless public exposure in a public art display (*Alison Lapper Pregnant*) takes root in a longer artistic and personal process of "coming out" as a sexual, and indeed reproductive woman. As discussed previously, Lapper has compared Quinn's statue to these nude self-portraits. She remarks that she has never had trouble finding boyfriends, yet many proved to take advantage of and even abuse her, and she acknowledges that nonetheless, having specifically nondisabled partners was viewed by society as a normalizing triumph for her. Lapper also recognizes the discrepancy between the mainstream vision of her sexuality (or lack thereof) and her own self-image, stating, "My friends who are able-bodied confirm that most people consider it weird and perverse that anyone should find me sexually attractive."[39]

A quite different perspective of her sexuality and body image emerges in Lapper's artwork. For example, Lapper's *Untitled* (2000) features three views of her nude body in Venus-like, s-curve poses. The photographic media articulates her musculature, flesh, and curve of the breast, while aestheticizing equally her upper-arm "stumps." The strong contrasts of the black background with the marble whiteness of her skin create a photographic sculpture in the round. The photograph, like Duffy's performance and Quinn's work, plays with the viewer's recognition of Classical statuary, particularly a goddess of love (and fertility), and the disabled flesh, as well as perceptions of "whole" versus "deficient" bodies. Carving the sculpture in the round refers specifically to Classical methods of producing balanced, proportional "wholes," a symbolic practice quoted also by feminist performance artist Eleanor Antin in *Carving: A Traditional Sculpture* (July 15, 1972–August 21, 1972), in which the artist documented her body from all sides daily, as it gradually reduced during a crash diet. Antin's photographs are formally clinical in their starkness, referring to the "before" and "after" photographs quite familiar in our makeoverobsessed contemporary culture, while her body becomes a piece of sculpture in characteristic practices of performance art (such as in the work of Gilbert and George). Particularly to twenty-first-century eyes, Antin's images refer to eating disorders and the extents women will go to "perfect" their bodies, according to increasingly narrow and impossible social standards for beauty. Lapper's and Antin's photographic sculptures in the round, like Quinn's sculptures, expose the notion of the "ideal" as fabricated. Lapper's work especially presents a certain disruption between artistic and social visions of the ideal and anti-ideal female body.

Art has provided a means for Lapper to interrogate the relationships between others' and her own images of her body and to reinvent her image in the public eye. These themes continued in her 2000 exhibit at the Fabrica Gallery in Brighton, a collection that featured sculptural works and photographs of Lapper from childhood to adulthood. The photographs intentionally crossed genres, including artistic self-portraits, snapshots taken by friends at key moments in Lapper's life, and early childhood medical photographs, which questioned viewer's assumptions about viewing her body in different visual contexts. The inclusion of medical photographs in particular was meant to disarm the viewer and incorporate, as well as intervene on, Lapper's experiences of feeling like a medical spectacle and specimen. Other works in the show featured Lapper's face in the vintage black and white style of photographs of classic Hollywood starlets. These images were strategically placed in a frame on the floor and covered in salt crystals. The viewer had to kneel down and brush aside the crystals to see Lapper's face, portrayed in a photographic softness reminiscent of glamour shots, which was intended to offset the hard-edged format of the medical images. The demand for viewer interaction with these works, as well at their themes of veiling, revealing, and concealing the body, make them performative—another public display of the disabled body.

Lapper strives in this work to showcase the disabled body as artistic and worthy of aestheticized display. Also featured at the Fabrica were photographic collages, with added elements such as flowers and angel wings that symbolized Lapper's biographical and artistic journeys. In Lapper's *Angel* (1999), now owned by the Brighton Museum, Lapper's head and nude torso in black and white project from the right edge of the colored frame. She bears wings and the body thrusts upward, soaring, like the winged messenger god, Hermes, or the confident, yet tragic Icarus, to unforeseen heights of knowledge and personal vistas. Winged figures, from Classical mythology to contemporary fantasy, transverse the heavens and the earth—the realms of the gods and mortals; they are figures with extraordinary bodies and supernatural abilities for travel. Like the disfigured artists featured in Chapter 1, Lapper incarnates goddess imagery, enacting a revision of art history and resurgence of the disabled body in shameless, empowered self-display. She appropriates allegorical bodies to frame her own, in specifically embodied and personally invested displays. In this frame, *Angel* invokes also the winged Nike, the mythical personification of victory, who is sometimes depicted bearing wings in the place of arms (as in the monumental, Hellenistic *Nike of Samothrace*, (c.190 CE)). The Nike form is poignantly a derivative of Athena, the goddess known for her protection of the city of Athens and is venerated still today at the Parthenon, the original home of *The Elgin Marbles*. Athena, or Minerva as she was known by the Romans, was a single mother and the goddess of wisdom, women's deeds, and the arts—a quite fitting allegory for Lapper to embody. Further, as Warner (1985) describes, Athena shape-shifted to a number of personas and bodies in order to invoke powers and enact deeds. These performative masquerades of the goddess included her strategic exposure and concealment of her body and identity. Like Athena's performances, Lapper's self-portrait works reveal and conceal her body in multiplying references and significances; similarly to *Alison Lapper Pregnant*, Lapper's bodywork is pregnant with meaning.

Lapper's works, like Quinn's, juxtapose the portrayal of the body as symbolic allegory and as a portrait subject. As an allegorical figure, *Alison Lapper Pregnant* follows in a tradition of staging the female body particularly as a symbol of heroic, virtuous, and largely patriarchal social values. Justice, Prudence, Fortitude, and Temperance, for examples, are values embodied by the female allegory of British history, Britannia, a Neoclassical figure derived from Athena and featured most prominently in Neoclassical design on Roman-inspired British coins. The Classical Roman revival in Britain, which inspired the architecture and figurative program of Trafalgar Square, appealed to traditions of piety, austerity, and humility of British society, social ideals upheld still today across the British political, social, and economic landscapes. *Alison Lapper Pregnant*, as a Neoclassical sculpture in the round, brings to life the corporeal elements of metaphysical allegories. Lapper's arch defiance of such longstanding conservative ideals, however, radiates from the sparkling surface of her body and tells "other" stories of British citizenship. She both conforms to and reforms stereotypes of disability, as well as of the British "public." Lapper's self-portrait photographs present additionally graphic portrayals of her particularized experiences, while co-opting the powers of infamous female beings. Britannia follows in the legacy of Athena as the civic goddess and as a symbol of law-abiding chastity; as a reincarnation of these goddesses, Lapper gives birth to new histories of the Square and the British nation, both by posing for the statue and producing self-representations.

Lapper has expressed mixed feelings about the connection between her own work and Quinn's. She was reluctant to pose for Quinn because she questioned the likeness of his work to her own, which has not been funded adequately enough to do such monumental, marble works and has not received the same attention as his work. She has admitted feeling a bit resentful, wondering if the public would ever take the same notice of a disabled artist, and she has doubted that she can continue her work in the shadows of Quinn's. But then she realized the importance of the public piece nonetheless and felt honored to be a part of it.[40] Her role in the narration of *Alison Lapper Pregnant* has brought a voice to its depiction of a pregnant amputee woman, as well as of a contemporary artist; Lapper's own work, which has experienced more attention, albeit slowly, contributes to significant dialogues and representations of disability in visual culture, both today and historically. Adrian Searle (2005) of the *Guardian* has eloquently expressed the impact of viewing Quinn's statue alongside Lapper's self-representations:

> Marc Quinn's *Alison Lapper Pregnant* is a much more arresting, impressive and strange work than photographs can convey. Even Alison Lapper's own naked, photographic self-portraits do not really prepare you for the sculpture itself. . . . Once seen, it is hard to drag one's eyes away. It isn't just the size and mass of Quinn's sculpture, or the cool, off-white marble, lighter than any of the stone of the square or the buildings around it. It is all in the form, and the strangeness of Alison Lapper's body itself, its irreducible familiarity and otherness. . . . Perhaps we needed the example of Picasso's portraits to recognise beauty in certain faces. And it could be that the model of Picasso's eroticised, biomorphic figures of the 1920s and 30s also allow us to see that Alison Lapper can be beautiful too, in the same way that Velasquez's portraits of dwarfs remind us of the humanity of his subjects.[41]

This viewer articulates the effects of the dialogues created between Quinn's and Lapper's works and the many artistic traditions they both invoke, from Classical to Modern. Quinn's and Lapper's images cause the viewer to do a double take and to perceive bodies on display in different lights and with frameworks outside of the strict conventions of social ideals. These artists call into question the integrity of Neoclassicism and other idealizing and/or disfiguring traditions for displaying the body in art, as well as in everyday life. Searle's quote also illuminates, as this chapter has emphasized, the necessity of placing the works of disabled and nondisabled artists in dialogues with each other and with art history, in order to see art history through new eyes and from the perspective *of* disability. In collaboration, such dialogues can forge fresh, multidimensional images of disability in the public eye, and potentially, can sculpt new, liberating body ideals for the public.[42]

# 3

# Performing Amputation

Joel-Peter Witkin's *Humor and Fear* (1999) stages a young amputee model in a theatrical, pseudo-antique scene. The image embodies seemingly disparate genres for representing the body: artistic, theatrical, medical, and freakish. She is posed nude on a pedestal or chest that resembles a Classical sarcophagus with its figurative sculptural program, and leans on one arm and hip, with her other arm raised to display of a small bowl. Her posture is unnatural for a portrait subject, as her body becomes embedded in an allegorical program, like the ones carved into her pedestal. Surrounded by vegetal props that resemble a Greek entablature motif, the model is framed within a curved, darkened background that creates a proscenium arch—the symbol of Greek theater. This background, printed in painterly, heavy inks, contrasts with the glaring whites of her marblelike skin and sets off her illuminated body as a decorative sculptural, architectural, or still life object. The marks Witkin has applied to the plate and the sepia washes over the print give the photograph an additional antique aesthetic. The model resembles a generic art historical nude, yet the photograph emphasizes the tangible materiality of her graphically naked, explicit body. The photographic medium highlights the texture of her flesh and pubic hair, which surpasses the illusion of marble and her possible symbolic connotations; with scientific accuracy, the photograph emphasizes the tactility of the scene. The folds in her skin pair visually with the folds in an animated drapery that surrounds her body, climbs over one arm, and seems to have a life of its own, again contrasting with and highlighting the static, inanimate pose of the model.

The qualities of "humor" and "fear" articulated by the title allude to its many paradoxes. The photographic frame and the numerous ambiguous details contribute to a multigenre and infinitely suggestive tableau. The model dons a bra made of translucent plastic cones that—reveal her erect nipples, emphasizing the materiality of her eroticized body. As a female body on display, partially nude to emphasize her nakedness, she is sexually objectified. Yet, the artificiality and excessive details, bordering on ridiculous, subtract this scene from a history of complicit and/or alluring female bodies on display for consumption by the viewer. Her profile displays a pointy costume nose, another common feature that is broken in antique sculpture, yet here resembling more of a Halloween mask, paired with Mickey Mouse ears. The humor of the scene is combined with its elements of fear, as the hybrid image juxtaposes seeming opposites. This title raises many questions, including whose "humor and fear" surround this body and its excessive photographic display—the model's, the viewers', or Witkin's?

Despite the plethora of visual detail, the viewer's eyes are drawn to the sites of the model's impairments. The amputated stumps and "deformed" hands become objectified, like other parts of her costumed body, or fetishized, a theme which some scholars have found as characteristic of photographs of disabled bodies. Garland-Thomson (2000) maintains that such fetishization of the body, derived from medical models, serves to eclipse the multidimensional nature of disabled subjects, constructing disability as social spectacle.[1] In these frameworks, the image's "offering" is an opportunity to gaze/stare at the amputee, and the book in which this photograph is featured satisfies the viewer's consequential desire to know "what happened" to make the body abnormal. The diagnostic text paired with the photograph states that the model lost her limbs as a young woman, due to toxic shock syndrome incurred from the use of a tampon, a modern day source of fear and danger for women.[2] She has been amputated by medical procedures and as a consequence of using an implement marketed to women. Medicine has impaired her, as does this constructed image of her body. The scientific rendering of her body in photographic detail adds to her role as a medical specimen, subjected to a diagnostic gaze/stare. Yet Witkin's compositions refuse conformity to such predictable implications in their dramatic displays of the disabled body.

The image exceeds medical discourses in its blatant theatricality, and the artist's personal touch on the photographic plate disrupts the illusion that photography produces and reproduces its subject scientifically. Witkin blows up the negatives of representation, so to speak, as he serves up the disabled body on a platter. In this and all of Witkin's work, the fetishization of the body is fully sensationalized and made into a theatrical spectacle—fetishized bodies are spotlighted, placed on pedestals, and framed in excessive stage sets, which further exaggerates how all photography may be said to solicit a stare. Perhaps problematically, she is not posed to stare back at the viewer, which further objectifies her. In the image, her face is only half exposed as she turns away from the viewer's gaze and stares beyond the frames of the image, perhaps in refusal to allow unlimited voyeuristic access to her body or to protect herself from a diagnostic stare. Or perhaps she turns away in shame for her bodily "tragedy" or from the perverse exploitation and objectification of her body in the photograph and in visual traditions throughout history. And yet, the caption also introduces the model as a former gymnast and nude dancer prior to her illness—activities intensely centered on body display. The model therefore may be quite comfortable in settings of bodily display and has indeed elected to pose for the artist. Witkin has said that the model responded to the finished photograph with pride, expressing that it made her feel beautiful.[3] The excessive image frames how the amputee model's body exceeds classifications and conventions of visual genres. The photograph intervenes on what the viewer may think they know about representation and about the disabled body. It strategically fools the eye. Her stumps appear photographically amputated in the image, as if Witkin has surgically removed them, causing the viewer to do a double take. The image becomes a performance of amputation, on the parts of the model and the artist.

Witkin's photographs of amputees, in which he removes limbs photographically or fetishizes the sites of amputation visually, offer a superlative example of how his photographic techniques dismember multiple histories of bodily display. Witkin dissects and sutures visual genres, such as art history, popular culture, pornography, dramatic and medical theaters, medical photography, and freak show displays. He focuses on the visual conventions with which these genres display the body, and specifically, how they produce the disabled or "abnormal" body as spectacle. In these acts of amputation, Witkin challenges the assumed unity or integrity of artistic conventions, as well as social standards for bodily appearance. The images glorify physical "abnormality" and disfigurement. They stage the amputee body in particular as an aesthetic object, objectifying and perhaps dehumanizing the models. Yet the photographs, like the bodies they feature, exceed conventions through dynamic framings and excessive displays. Witkin's works are extreme at the site of carnal extremities. These corporeal tableau vivants have been characterized as too perverse, too blasphemous, too excessive, or in general, too grotesque, and for many, his framing of disability is one of his most offensive orchestrations.[4] Yet, I argue that rather than objectifying the disabled, here amputee body, one-dimensionally, Witkin explodes the potential significances of his models' bodies, as they refuse conformity to two-dimensional representations. His images serve as stages on which amputees parade their corporeal spectacularity.

Witkin corrupts visual histories of bodily display more so than he corrupts the models' bodies within them. Specifically, Witkin amputates the medium of photography and its historical associations with the medical gaze. Photography's presumed depiction of objective reality equates the medium with scientific accuracy and medical precision.[5] Innovations in photography have enabled graphic depiction of the corporeal body and have increased visual access to it. Early photographers were considered technicians rather than artists, and many clinical photographers were in fact physicians. However, Witkin manipulates this quality specifically by altering the flesh of his photographs in pseudosurgical techniques. By "doctoring" the images and performing amputation, Witkin reveals the intersections of artistic, social, and medical gazes at the disabled body. His blatant and significantly anesthetized objectification of amputee bodies elucidates the more deceptive objectification practices of clinical photography in particular, in which amputees and so-called disfigured others were frequently represented and medically pathologized. Witkin poignantly pairs the conventions of medical imagery with the traditions and motifs of Classical art, which serve as a legacy in Western culture for ideal beauty in art and other visual media. Compared with technical nature of clinical photography, Witkin performs photographic alchemy, clouding the distinctions between the real and the representational, science and art, and thereby revealing an inherent theatricality and freakishness of photography.

## Medical Curiousities

Witkin appropriates a conventional medical gaze. He draws much of his subject matter, particularly bodies and body fragments from medical laboratories, and has pursued long-term interest and artistic influence from historical medical exhibits, particularly ophthalmologist Stanley B. Burns' collection of early medical photographs,[6] from which I will draw specific comparisons to Witkin's own photographs. Witkin's work shares many qualities with early medical images, including themes of photography and medicine as scientifically "objective" and/or objectifying, especially as constructed through aesthetic form; imagery of death (*Teatro de Morte* [1989]) and illness (*John Herring: Person with AIDS Posed as Flora with Lover* [New Mexico] [1992]); dissection (*Still Life with Mirror* [1998] and *Anna Akhmatova* [1998]) and other surgical practices and medical devices (*Un Santo Oscuro* [1987]; representation of skeletal anatomy (*Who Naked Is* [1996]); display of fetuses (*Hermes* [1981]), particularly with fatal intrauterine anomalies; and images of what may be termed living human curiosities or pathological cases, many of which may be considered disabled (such as in numerous Witkin images of amputees). The body forms characteristically featured in medical exhibits, clinical photography, and Witkin's contemporary photography are bodies marked as curious by birthmarks, atypical anatomical growths (*Art Deco Lamp* [1986]), disfigurements (*Abundance* [1997]), or evidence of disease; homosexuals (*Queer Saint* [1999]); so-called hysterics and the insane; and bodies staged as monsters and freaks historically in curiosity cabinets, festivals, public markets (*Portrait of a Dwarf* [1987]), and freak show displays (*Melvin Burkhart, Human Oddity* [1985]). These subjects, in the context of medicine and other spectacle displays, are framed as medical curiosities, united only by their excessive corporealities and physical transgressions from the norm.

Witkin's photographs, through their exaggerations and excesses, call attention to the deceptively sanitized voyeurism of the medical gaze. Human "anomalies and curiosities" have fascinated medicine for centuries; they have been exhibited in medical texts and collections, in two-dimensional forms and live presentations. Renaissance physician Ambroise Paré's iconic *On Monsters and Marvels* (1840),[7] an illustrated example of collected case studies and diagnoses (many supernatural) of abnormal bodies, fantastical creatures, and other environmental natural phenomena, reads like a natural history text and has been cited by scholars as precedence for the modern freak show and other medical displays.[8] Similarly to Paré's text, nineteenth-century physicians' George Gould and Walter Pyle's *Anomalies and Curiosities of Medicine* (1896) (contemporary with early medical photography such as Burns' collection, as well as the nineteenth- and early twentieth-century heyday of the freak show) is a medical text that illustrates convergences of empiricism and voyeurism, reality and myth, and clinical explanation and mythology.[9] It struggles to classify its diverse "anomalies and curiosities," and becomes a survey of menagerie "others."[10] Numerous case studies in this volume are popular freak show performers, and it provides minimal diagnostic information, but seems rather preoccupied by exhibitionism and freakishness.

Early medical photography likewise often turned its gaze on freaks, a widely popular form of entertainment in the nineteenth to early twentieth century in the United States and Europe (approximately 1830s–1930s) (*Lucia Zarate, the Mexican Lilliputian* [c. 1880]), and illustrated informational and promotional freak show materials to establish wondrous freaks as real and believable for paying customers. Perhaps ironically, the medical models that pathologized such bodies contributed to the demise of the freak show as an acceptable form of public entertainment. The freak show provides a strong example of representational collisions between art, science, and popular entertainment in performances of the disabled body, qualities shared with Witkin's staging of amputees particularly. Witkin's work shares with medicine a preoccupation with curious or abnormal bodies, and his medical gaze is likewise voyeuristic and theatrical. Witkin's camera is also attracted to freaks (*Melvin Burkhart, Human Oddity* [1985]), today relegated to subcultural venues such as Coney Island, but highlights their wondrous bodies as spectacular and performative rather than medically legitimate. Whereas medicine gazed at curiosities as examples against which to define and medically administer a preferred state of a "normal" or healthy body, Witkin celebrates bodily deviance from the norm.

Witkin's hybrid images, like *Humor and Fear*, compare thematically with historical medical theaters, which combined genres of visual and performing arts, science, and popular entertainment in their staging of the body as spectacle. Further, the discourses on the body and bodily representations produced by medical theaters have served as a legacy for the conventions of representing the body in art, science, and the freak show. Flourishing in the Renaissance and continuing to modern times, public dissections and anatomy studies are at the heart of figurative art historically, influencing how the body has been depicted in painting, sculpture, and photography.[11] In addition, these medical spectacles strongly influenced modern notions of "normal" versus "abnormal," or pathological, anatomy, which was conceived of specifically in opposition to the Classical ideal.[12] Such designations then served in the ranking of society and individuals, creating hierarchies of individual and social bodies. Witkin's photographs traffic in these intersections of visual culture and the consequences of representation for real social subjects, particularly by juxtaposing the medically "abnormal" with the Classical ideal.

### Dissecting Norms and Conventions

Witkin's subjects, like Quinn's, challenge notions of ideal versus anti-ideal bodies. Disability studies theorist Lennard J. Davis (1995) traces the concept of "normal" historically and its implication for disabled people,[13] arguing that normal is a culturally specific social construct that privileges homogeneity and stigmatizes those with physical differences. Normal is distinctively abstract, disembodied, and defined only in opposition to the intensely embodied and spectacularized abnormal body. Davis insists that normal, from the nineteenth century to the present, designates an ideal body image and that deviation from the norm, such as disability represents, becomes deviant. Further, Davis draws parallels between modern notions of normal to earlier, Classical ideals for the body. These Classical models were most clearly expressed in the 450 BCE Canon of Polykleitos, which established an ideal body type, derived from mathematical proportions and the most aesthetic parts drawn from different individuals. Polykleitis's prescription for the ideal corresponded to a sculptural figure that embodied geometric precision and ration and conveyed "wholeness" through symmetry and balance. Such rigid parameters continue to serve as the benchmark for corporeal beauty in art and, as Davis argues, influence social standards for appearance, up to present day. The elevation of normal as a physical ideal in the nineteenth century resulted from a constellation of social discourses in literature, statistics, eugenics, and Social Darwinism, Davis maintains, and this construction of normal posited disability as the pathological opposite to be cured or eliminated from the population. Davis's theories provide a means to equate social and artistic conventions for bodies when interpreting Witkin's photographs, while Witkin's photographs illuminate the leading role of photography in Davis's arguments.

Photography is indeed the additional coordinate to Davis historiography of normal versus abnormal. Nineteenth-century photography produced visual images of pathology and deviance, both corporeal and moral, against which mainstream society could assure their own normality.[14] These photographs contributed to the diagnosing of, and gave a visual image to such "abnormality." One of the first uses of photography in the nineteenth century was for documentation of patients for medical records, education, and media publication. Clinical portraits of patients, such as *World War I Soldier with Amputated Leg*, have functioned historically not only to document, but also to legitimize the still somewhat suspect medical profession in the nineteenth century for potential patients, or society at large. The association of photography with science was a key attribute for medical use of the medium in constructing its public image and legitimacy. Because photography was considered objective in its depiction of reality and establishment of evidence, these photographs presented supposed objective and true representations of the body, communicated specifically through strict visual conventions. The images characteristically capture live human bodies with an aesthetic and discursive detachment, by framing a frontal or profile image of the face or full body against a generally indistinguishable backdrop. This kind of voided background, like a natural history illustration, symbolizes a void of context or lack of personal identification of the subject portrayed. Often, handwritten identification numbers referring to hospital records and brief clinical diagnoses served as textual landscapes in the photographs. A few inanimate objects, or props, were sometimes included in more formal portraitlike compositions, to present further classification of the patient by social class and diagnosis. The subject was in general classified according to their pathology: disease, impairment, or other curious feature. These images, through composition and technique, composed a "whole" or unified image of pathology. Such photographs established medical authority over the body and constructed an image of medicine and of the pathologized, medical body for the public.

The amputee veteran featured in *World War I Soldier with Amputated Leg* poses according to the conventions for depicting veterans, who were characteristically afforded more dignity and portraitlike distinction than other subjects in order to represent their historical status as national heroes.[15] Centered in the frame, he stands alone in his identifying uniform, as the photograph is absent of other elements that could distinguish him. Poignantly, the uniform is fragmented on the so-called fragmented man, who is naked from the waist down, revealing much more than his one amputated leg. In a different medium, his static body would resemble Classical sculpture. In the photograph he becomes medicalized, specimenlike, and objectified, similarly to the *stilled life* of a stiff life composition, a look which is characteristic of nineteenth-century photographic techniques, as lengthy exposure time, for example, and other technological elements contributed to the appearance of bodies themselves as inanimate objects. Life is here stilled (immobilized), in posture and discursive framing. The half-naked soldier with an amputated leg then becomes an "amputee," or further, a dehumanized personification of amputation. The soldier is here a depersonalized manifestation of pathology or tragedy, despite that he is more than metaphorically and illusionistically alive. In contrast with many clinical subjects whose eyes were blocked or shielded, this soldier's face is uncovered and his eyes revealed to meet the viewer's and physician's gazes; yet, nonetheless, he is objectively revealed for examination and diagnosis as a possession of science—both his unsightly, amputated stump and his penis exposed to the gaze. The soldier, despite his display of virility, is emasculated photographically.

Many clinical images objectified their subjects by blocking their eyes, a technique which Witkin's images subvert particularly as he subverts the assumed neutrality of the medical gaze. Technicians (many of whom were physicians) blocked the eyes when developing the image, or covered the face of the subject with a veil or blindfold, making the body anonymous for the benefit of the patient *and* the physician or other viewer, such that the subject could be examined with objective, impersonal disinterest. Shielding of the eyes was seen more predominantly in especially freakish or curious subjects and those of lower socioeconomic status.[16] This technique provided far more protection for the viewer of the photograph than the subject, however, for this blocking of the eyes, meant to maintain the patients' dignity, functioned rather to impose shame and impeded a returned gaze, preventing the patients' agency as individuals to transcend the medical frame. Witkin subverts the blocking of the eyes with his subjects who wear masks, such as in *Humor and Fear*, and in images in which he scratches over the subject's eyes on the photographic plate, such as in *Hermes*, a horrific photograph of a decaying corpse playing the role of the Greek messenger god in a specific quotation of a famous sculpture by Praxiteles (Praxiteles, *Hermes and the Infant Dionysus*, likely a Hellenistic marble copy of a Roman bronze statue of the fourth century BCE). In Witkin's photographic version, the corporeality of the decomposing corpse and the worn look created with photographic alteration visually denote Classical ruin. In *Hermes*, Witkin's has blocked the body's eyes with heavy inking and removed the corpse's limbs. By altering the flesh of the body through the skin of the photograph, Witkin assumes the role of a surgeon. He intervenes on a so-called scientific gaze at the dismembered body, again by engaging and dissecting medical and Classical iconography.

Like *Hermes*, Witkin's *Portrait of Greg Vaughan* (2004) (Figure 3.1) also manipulates medical and Classical figurative traditions, yet by engaging a contemporary amputee subject. The nude model stands in static pose against a black and weathered-looking backdrop, quite similarly to the veteran featured in the clinical photograph. His delicate body exhibits the characteristic look of the adolescent or androgynous physique that was particularly idealized in Classical statuary. The early Greek ideal *kouros* figure (meaning young man) portrayed gods, warriors, and athletes in static poses derived from

**Figure 3.1** Joel-Peter Witkin, *Portrait of Greg Vaughan* (2004). Courtesy of the Catherine Edelman Gallery

Egyptian statues, which conveyed nobility and heroism. Unlike the soldier (also a hero), this modern day *kouros* in *Portrait of Greg Vaughan* is entirely nude (as the body is considered in art) and/or naked (as it is considered in medical imagery). He turns slightly to the left, in a subtle contrapposto—a curved pose developed by the Canon of Polykleitis to best display a perfect balance of weight-bearing and relaxed limbs and ideal physical proportions; for Greg Vaughan, this pose displays best to the viewer the site of his amputation. His right arm, which is "missing" in contrast to an assumed body standard and artistic canon of wholeness, resembles the familiar breakage of antique marble statues.

The photographic medium creates and simultaneously disrupts such an illusion. Like Quinn's *The Complete Marbles*, the model here embodies a historical shift in Classical sculpture from earlier portrayals of the gods to later, Hellenistic sculptures of mortal life, specifically in expressions of high drama. The image is theatrical. Witkin brings Classical sculpture to life, with photographic depiction of mortal flesh. The photograph's trompe l'oeil effect, the "fooling of the eye" in art historical vocabulary, is theatrically exaggerated by the pasty whiteness of the model's skin, which makes Greg Vaughan look as though he were being cast in plaster—a material that crosses art and medical use, as well as his seeming attachment the pedestal behind him. This kind of merging of the body with a marble support is characteristic of Roman copies of Greek hollow-cast bronzes (like Praxiteles' *Hermes*). It also suggests Greek statues that are architectural remains, like the figures "in antis" (figures that served as pillars), such that the body was originally part of, as well as embedded in an antique temple or mausoleum. By quoting the look of a body that has been cut out, or amputated, from a larger architectural program—emphasized in the photograph by the crown molding edges of the pedestal and its rougher, rocky top—the photograph, like *Humor and Fear*, plays with visions of the body *with* and *as* ornamental objects. The image also recalls an Impressionist work by Auguste Rodin, who was known for adopting Classical imagery, such as bodily fragmentation and inclusion of supports, in his quite modern work. Like Witkin, Rodin incorporated finger marks as the artist's personal, impressionistic touch. In *Portrait of Greg Vaughan*, the berries depicted like a crown on the body's head, a still life element included also in *Humor and Fear*, hint at associations with Dionysus (as he was known to the Greeks) or Bacchus (to the Romans), the god of wine who symbolizes, from ancient to contemporary culture, the celebration of earthly and bodily pleasures. This crown may also refer to the laurel wreaths characteristic of figures of Apollo specifically and athletes in general to signify victory, suggesting Greg Vaughan's limber finesse. The photograph subverts both Classical and Neoclassical representations of the body and the productions of "ideal" and "normal" bodies in artistic and medical images. Also like Quinn, Witkin has designated the image as a portrait of a specific man: this is "Greg Vaughan," not just a generic *kouros* or anonymous soldier. The image strategically creates perceptual confusions between the portrait subject and the symbolic object, between flesh and marble.

Witkin's images of Classicized amputees intervene on how a viewer reads so-called objective representations of the body in scientific rendering, as well as in the ideals of art. Placing photographs such as *Humor and Fear* and *Portrait of Greg Vaughan* alongside the naked amputee veteran in *World War I Soldier with Amputated Leg* provides a poignant comparison that prompts the viewer to look again, and differently, at the soldier's body. The visual pairing in the medical photograph of an amputated stump next to an anatomical symbol of masculine potency allows the lauded soldier to escape emasculation—amputation is visually differentiated from castration. He becomes a disabled hero, rather than a gross specimen or victim. The clinical image mediates the body and its social status. He raises his uniform, enhancing his nakedness and proudly displaying his virility—he is half-exposed, half-objectified, perhaps like Greg Vaughan in corporeal fusing with an object pedestal. The soldier's body is constructed in the clinical photograph as half normal and half broken. The soldier is half erotically concealed and half revealed, pornographically, through medical exposure.[17] The halves are not lacking in these images, but in juxtaposition, exceed the meanings of a so-called unified, cohesive, or "whole" image. The soldier stands firm on his one leg, its stability and fortitude highlighted in the photograph. This photograph now not only represents, but performs amputation similarly to *Humor and Fear* and *Portrait of Greg Vaughan*, not as a surgical and disarming act of removing limbs, but rather as an embodied performance of identity.

Witkin's photographic performances of amputation dissect the inherent contradictions, supposed neutrality, and integrity of the medical gaze and medical imagery. He defies medical traditions by manipulating photographic conventions specifically. Scholars of photography have argued that such specific conventions produced a portrait image of pathology in society,[18] thus contributing to racist, classicist, and sexist ideologies.[19] I would add ablest to this list. These prejudices, definitions of pathology, and social systems that upheld them were justified through the photographs, whose supposed "neutrality" and integrity were actually mechanically constructed. Adherence to the strict rules of convention in early photographs secured the truth conveyed in documentation. Departing from convention could undermine the "truths" about the body they were meant to convey. Consequentially, irregularities in photographic conventions and techniques (abnormalities or deviance of the image itself in comparison with other clinical images) were strategically altered to produce a unified look of pathology and deviance; Photographers purposefully subtracted any trace of chance circumstance, the artist's imprint, or personal touch, to avoid deviation from convention and to therefore make their images more scientific and believable.[20]

Witkin's careful altering to achieve the look of nineteenth-century photography affiliates his work with early scientific images, ironically. In contrast to the seemingly sanitized or unified appearance of medical images to convey "pathology," Witkin's hands-on techniques and personal touch makes his images decidedly unscientific, subjective, and even theatrical. He executes intensive and laborious alterations to his plates and images, including scratching into the surface, printing over areas of the body, tedious processes with encaustic beeswax, hand polishing, bleaching, and hand painting of the print. He sometimes literally dissects and sutures negatives with an exacto knife. Sepia washes in particular make the images appear yellowed and worn, as in *Humor and Fear*, replicating the photographic practices and look of nineteenth-century photography. Many of Witkin's photographs resemble daguerreotypes and other forms of early photography, or significantly, how they appear reprinted for today's audience of viewers. In these acts, he dissects the conventions of and distinctions between art and scientific representation. In the process, he undermines the authority of images to mediate the body through its conventional and aesthetic display. The images call attention to the contradictions inherent to clinical imagery by revealing their strategic spectacularization of so-called abnormal bodies. Witkin makes vivid how bodies are never neutral in representation, but always altered mechanically through his surgical practices and visual dismemberment.

## Fragmented and Fetishized Bodies

For many viewers, Witkin's acts of fragmentation are disarming, even violent, for he fragments the body and visual history. The fragmented body in representation conventionally portrays a "broken" or deficient body and, in contemporary art in particular, often symbolizes psychic or societal fragmentation through corporeal defect. Witkin, by contrast, produces excessive compositions that provide excesses of meaning and potentials for interpretation. The visual fragment is not forever lacking in Witkin's fetishizing frames, but rather, oversignified, specifically in the already fragmented, already oversignified medium of photography.

Mexican painter Frida Kahlo's visual and symbolic fragmentation, or fetishization, of her disabled body illuminates the significances of Witkin's work, particularly by adding perspectives of disability. Kahlo's use of bodily elements, particularly blood and interior female anatomy, was influenced by medical illustration,[21] such that her work shares with Witkin's fascination with medical imagery. The prominent presence of dismembered feet in her work, as well as her many images of her body in pieces, equate with Witkin's imagery further. In Kahlo's paintings, feet bear especially multivalent references to Mexican votive symbols (*milagros*, or objects that embody and evoke miracles), such as a dismembered hand-shaped earring she models in *Self-Portrait* (1940). These feet also reference her own personal history, particularly her physical impairments, including an early limp from polio and injuries from her accident that she struggled with her entire life, eventually resulting in the amputation of one foot.

Kahlo's *What the Water Gave Me* (1938) frames the artist's gaze at herself fragmented in the bathtub. The viewer, through Kahlo's gaze, sees the story of her life and her art floating around prominent images of her legs, which are dismembered by the top frame of the painting. A collage of visual fragments drawn from her many paintings (consisting primarily of autobiographical portraits and still life scenes), the composition is a visual reflection of Kahlo's body and a mental reflection on her life, as well as her identity as a biracial, bisexual, and disabled woman. Surrounding veiled semblances of Kahlo's outstretched legs, numerous images rise to the surface of and sink in her murky bathwater. A lesbian, mixed-race couple lounges in sexual play on a sponge (a scene featured in Kahlo's *Two Nudes in a Forest* [1939]). Portraits of her parents (her German-American father and Mexican-Indian mother) from their wedding photograph emerge, as does a disembodied Mexican-Tehuana peasant dress Kahlo frequently wore and often modeled in her self-portraits. A conch shell lies broken and leaking, perhaps symbolizing flawed fertility and Kahlo's inability to bear children to term and a symbol she included in gruesome paintings of her numerous miscarriages, such as the *Henry Ford Hospital* (1932). An erupting phallic skyscraper seen here is drawn from Kahlo's early 1930s work, specifically paintings inspired by her visits to urban U.S. cities (New York and Detroit) while her husband, Diego Rivera, worked on famous mural commissions. Other images include a tiny, animated skeleton from popular Mexican Day of the Dead celebrations for spiritual ancestors, as well as a body representing death in a broader sense; a dead bird; and erotic flowers. A connecting cord, perhaps umbilical, strings together these floating metaphors, creating connections between Kahlo's body in pieces and pieces of her life history, memory, and fantasy.

Fragmented in the water—the fluid of life—Kahlo's body and this painted expression of it are pregnant with meaning, specifically in fluid, unfixed symbols with irresolvable signification. All the images surfacing in the water are tied to the fragmented body and touch upon, but do not completely dissolve into, Kahlo's identity as disabled. Her impairments are vividly represented at the top of the composition in two feet, only half emerging above the surface of the water; the right foot is bleeding, apparently wounded (as Kahlo's own feet caused her continuous pain), and both feet mirror themselves in the water to create surrealistic illusions of double-sided, anamorphic forms. In a different tone, Kahlo illustrated dismembered feet with sprouting roots in her diary, with the handwritten caption "Feet, what do I need them for when I have wings to fly"

(1953). In Kahlo's work and in comparisons with photographs of the body in pieces discussed in this chapter, feet prove impossible to contain in symbolic connotation, particularly in the conventions of art and science. These feet are oversignified fetishes, fetishized by the compositions.

Witkin's prominent inclusions and exclusions of feet also invoke the symbolism of the foot as fetish, playing with the contexts (art, science, and in addition, pornography) for viewing the body. The fetish already operates as a paradoxical concept as both a phallic symbol whose presence points to phallic absence, or more specifically, castration. Feet as sexual fetishes bear infinite cultural signification. Surrealist writer Georges Bataille has written that feet vary radically in reception and symbolism across cultures and time periods. Regarding the sexual allurement of the foot, it is a titillating symbol that embodies sin and deviance. Bataille proposes that because the foot is closer to the earth, it connotes the fall of man and his morality, as well as his mortality, and is therefore a symbol of death.[22] Finally, feet elicit humor and horror, or perhaps their absence may elicit these responses from Witkin's *Humor and Fear*, for example. Witkin's photographs such as *Feast of Fools* (1990) (Figure 3.2), *Still Life, Mexico* (1992), and *Still Life with Mirror* (1998) showcase dismembered feet, which are actual body parts Witkin has collected from medical morgues. They are medical specimens, which Witkin again perverts in excessive art historical display as animated, still life fetish objects. Witkin stages these feet in multireferential and contradictory compositions of carnality, hedonism, consumption, and fragmentation.

Witkin's still lifes with dismembered feet bear visual similarities to the photograph that graces the cover and provides the title of Stanley Burns' photography book, *A Morning's Work* (1856) (by physician Reed B. Bontecou), a clinical image that features a pile of feet, amputated from soldiers, on a plate.[23] The title of the photograph hints at the characteristic detachment or disinterest of the medical gaze, despite the horror and reminders of human loss and war elicited by the image. The tactility of the parts, captured through the medium of photography, makes the scene graphic, both visually and emotionally. Witkin capitalizes on this ability of photography and combines lifelike, yet dismembered feet with still life and fantastical props (such as a squid, rotting and sliced-open

**Figure 3.2**   Joel-Peter Witkin, *Feast of Fools* (1990). Courtesy of the Catherine Edelman Gallery

fruit, and a fetal corpse in *Feast of Fools*), also captured in vivid, even entrancing detail. *A Morning's Work* and *Feast of Fools* juxtapose art and medical imagery, both desirable and repulsive, and they solicit strong and conflicting reactions from the viewer, raising countless symbolic and visceral associations.

Witkin's themes of feet and the amputation of them, like Kahlo's painted imagery, imbue the body in pieces—the fragmented body—with an excess of symbolism. Further, they provoke embodied, subjective reactions from the viewer. Bodily fragmentation and themes of amputation in these works offer up body images that resist representational closure and reject the idea of symbolic "wholes," as the fragment serves to embody infinite potentials. All representation, especially photographic, may be characterized as fragmentary, as pictures offer a moment or body stilled, a time or scene already passed away, manipulated, and dramatized through the very act of making it an image. Representations always fail to capture the "whole," for always, beyond the frame, there exists an excess that the viewers' eyes cannot see. Witkin's photographs frame his viewers' simultaneous desire for and exclusion from the image, specifically through his excessive bodily displays, in which "more is more." They leave the viewer gorged, and yet insatiate.

The argument that Witkin pushes the envelope too far is a strong one, as he perverts so-called photographic objectivity into a blatant and unashamed objectification of his own. Witkin's work has been largely criticized for tasteless display and exploitation of bodies for shock value. Witkin's camera is said to fetishize, capitalize on, and even contribute to human suffering.[24] He makes a strong statement about artistic traditions and the exhibitionism of medicine, yet at what costs? Witkin partakes in the historical exploitation and may practice his own form of dehumanization, particularly of disabled bodies. A problematic photograph in this vein is *Leo* (1976), part of the *Evidences of Anonymous Atrocities* series, which features an amputee man whose head is blurred over (a clinical reference?), appearing like a black leather mask. His suspenders resemble bondage straps, and he sits in cagelike armature. The body is not only framed as a nonhuman, inanimate object, but further, as a feral beast. Such display of the racialized, as well as the disabled body, as animalistic has roots also in the freak show, in the examples of developmentally disabled "missing links" and presentations of individuals with limb impairments or other disfigurements, such as the "Lobster Boy" or the "Elephant Man." The photograph's shadowing makes Leo's skin appear darker, suggesting he is an eroticized and subjugated image of a racial "other," or perhaps articulating, even mocking the social stereotypes that nonwhite, particularly African-American and Mexican men are criminal and violent. These dark overtones are accentuated by the fact that Leo has no legs, a characteristic of deviance or abnormality that Witkin capitalizes on to make the portrait ambiguously sadomasochistic or eerie. Leo might be a subject of social oppression, articulated by Witkin's photograph, yet does the image further oppress this man, or the woman in *Humor and Fear*, for that matter? Do these representations of amputees as objects problematically aestheticize disability, as a marginalized identity, and reinstate the representation of the disabled body as freakish "other"?

The use of a Classical, Western aesthetic may literally whitewash the various politics of representation. This charge has been waged against the late photographer Robert Mapplethorpe, whose Classicized photographs of a black man in *Ajitto* (four portraits from 1981), like Witkin's, fetishize socially marked and exploited bodies. The crouched and curled, almost fetal-like pose of the model in the *Ajitto* series, photographed from all sides like a specimen, recalls the figure's pose in a Neoclassical painting—Jean Hippolyte Flandrin, *Young Man Sitting by the Seashore* (1836). Significantly, this pose was repeated in a composition titled *Cain* (1900) by photographer Wilhelm von Gloedon, who specialized in Classical-themed, homoerotic pornography, as well as by photographer Fred Holland Day in *Negro Nude* (1900). The pose therefore bears a deep history tied to visually sexualized and racialized male bodies. Mapplethorpe's contemporary version, a series of homoerotic, pseudopornographic art photographs, makes the black male body into a sculptural object (in pose and lack of returned gaze), which problematically aestheticizes the model's exploitation.[25] The black body is photo*graphically* articulated—glistening against a completely white, or voided, background and pedestal. The photographs may confirm the normality of whiteness by fetishizing the black male body and therefore making it into an aesthetic object for possession. Peggy Phelan (1993) argues how these images reinstate the stereotype of the virile "stud," derived from slavery and minstrel traditions, particularly in Mapplethorpe's fetishization of the penis. In this interpretation, Classical conventions in Mapplethorpe's works "civilize" the naked black body, as well as the objectifying act of the photographer. Witkin's images of Classicized amputees may similarly engage Eurocentric and ableist conventions that effectively erase the power dynamics of the gaze/stare and deceptively mask his own photographic acts of exploitation.

Witkin's *Art Deco Lamp* (1985) serves as a rich example for interrogating his aesthetic acts, particularly with disfigured bodies. Here, the body of a woman with a hunchback kneels in a profile view and wraps her exceptionally arabesque body and elongated arm around a globe light. Her face is covered in a black mask, like Leo's, which raises identifications with prowlers and terrorists, yet here a clock face covers her human face to mask her gaze. The image duplicates an object from the period of Art Deco, an art, design, and decorative arts movement of Europe and later the United States from the turn of the century to the 1930s and 1940s, characterized by excessive patterning and ornament. The photograph recreates a popular Art Deco tradition of fusing a table lamp, often with such a globe light, with sculptural nude statues, particularly graceful, elongated dancers or curvy Neoclassical nymphettes. Such pieces stage the female body in and as a functional, domestic object, wherein the body becomes eroticized and aestheticized object for display. Witkin's witty take on this tradition may objectify this woman's body and disempower her, but he chose a design motif associated with excess and decadence specifically. The darkened background, treated with splashes of hand-applied wash and scratch marks, sets off her spotlighted torso, where the camera articulates her rounded breast, rib cage, and muscular arm and shoulder, behind which an unusual and shadowed concave area of the body curves into the bulge of her mythic, fabulous hump. The profile view best shows off this site of her disfigurement, which associates her with one of the most famously stigmatized and enfreaked figures of all time, Quasimodo. Quasimodo has become literature's and pop culture's quintessential deformed and ugly grotesque, a persona which Witkin's image of a hunchback contradicts. The hunchback here becomes an aesthetic and opulent object because her graceful body deviates from the norm. This model contacted Witkin and asked to be photographed, specifically in the nude. In her staging as a curious, indeed queer beauty, what role does Witkin play in what some viewers would call her aesthetic enfreakment?

### Freakish Displays

The showcasing of amputees as freaks has a long history that precedes and pervades Witkin's frames. In addition to documenting, diagnosing, and securing the legitimacy of "human curiosities," photographs also became souvenir portraits and marketing materials purchased by freak show patrons. One of the most collectible photographs was of the famous "Armless Wonder," Charles Tripp (1855–1939), who began exhibiting himself in P. T. Barnum's shows at age seventeen. Cartes de visites of Tripp visibly articulated his constructed persona as an "armless wonder"—freakish, yet admirable—by presenting the most domestic tasks and mundane pastime activities as extraordinary because of how he accomplished them with his visually fetishized feet. Tripp's performances consisted of particularly dexterous tasks, which highlighted his extraordinary ability to adapt or "overcome" his impairments. Historian Robert Bogdan (1988) describes Tripp's freak appearances: "Tripp's performance during his more than fifty years as an exhibit did not change much. He neither sang nor played a musical instrument but merely showed his patrons what he could do with his feet: carpentry, penmanship, portrait painting, paper cutting, and the like. At the turn of the century he took up photography."[26] An 1885 photograph of Tripp by Eisenmann presents a conventionalized portrait of a proper, almost normal Victorian gentleman wearing a distinguished suit, sitting upright on a pedestal surface, in the act of taking tea, except that the toes of his bare foot grasp the delicate china cup. Photographic portraits of "normal" Victorian men, like many clinical images, conventionally included props indicating their trade and status, as Tripp's props symbolize the content of his extraordinary performances, and here such props function to perform an ambivalent identity for a so-called proper, yet disabled man. A comb and brush set indicate that Tripp could miraculously groom and care for himself, making him efficient at specifically feminized tasks. The scissors, with which Tripp might cut out paper dolls (not exactly a "normal" task for a Victorian man) further feminized him as an amputee, an almost, half, or damaged man like a World War I veteran in the clinical image, gendered female according to his disabled, amputated body.

Tripp's creative acts were sentimentalized and trivialized, a theme that contrasts sharply with Witkin's freakish imagery. Tripp was known for writing, as evidenced by the inclusion of a pen and sample letter in the carte composition, and he engaged in additional creative acts—portrait painting and photography. At the turn of the century Tripp was billed as the "Armless Photographer," suggesting his extrasensory creative skills. Yet in the freak show, Tripp's body was the voyeuristic attraction, not his photographs. A compliment for how well he could write would have referred to how he manipulated a pen, not for the quality of his prose. Tripp's photographs did not capture attention beyond the freak show audience's interest in his body; his abnormal body and its abnormal means of handling the camera attracted the viewer's condescending patronage. Tripp's performance of specifically everyday, mundane and domestic tasks allowed viewers to identify with him while his undeniably abnormal body assured distance between the normal, nondisabled spectators and the disabled spectacle. In contrast, Witkin's images of amputees and other disfigured individuals do not ask for sentimentalized identification, nor pity. No attempts are made for his amputee models to masquerade as "normal," and certainly not in the performance of everyday life skills or tasks. On the contrary, the performances of amputees and amputation are excessively dramatic and even paranormal in Witkin's frames. The disfigured body becomes a work of art and source of creative powers.

The freak show indeed provides a historical precedence for contemporary disability theater and performance art, a legacy present in Witkin's photographs. For example, Witkin's *Gambler* (1986) (Figure 3.3) includes another fantastical and theatrical "amputee"

**Figure 3.3**  Joel-Peter Witkin, *Gambler* (1986). Courtesy of the Catherine Edelman Gallery

wearing a tuxedo, the white gloves of a magician, and a mask com-posed of five playing cards—perhaps a poker hand. He raises his left leg stump, uncovered by his shortened pants, as again Witkin's image provides a blatant opportunity to gaze/stare at his impaired body, offered up for the viewer. His other leg appears to be nor-mal, although intense bleaching and scratching at the bottom left of the photograph restricts full scrutiny of it. At the back of his right shoulder stands a bleached and scratched, framed object that morphs between a window pane and a mirror—collapsing two allegories for artistic representation as either a privileged sight into another world and/or a false reflection of reality. The mirror sug-gests also vanity, superficiality, and the duplicity of both the subject on display and the act of representation. This illusion that fools the eye in the photograph comments on the nature of representa-tion itself as illusionary, even delusional. The body dominates the composition, posed against a backdrop covered with an intensely geometric pattern, whose seeming lack of overall design program and enigmatic, disjunctive form sets the stage for visual mystery and interpretive riddle.

This composition has been compared to a tarot card image, making the disabled body clairvoyant and remarking on the vari-ous historical discourses of the abnormal body. Prior to increasing medicalization of such bodies in the eighteenth and nineteenth centuries, monsters, or children born with physical defects, such as congenital amputation, were said to be evidence of supernatu-ral warnings, embodiments of divine intervention, or phenomena caused by the powers of the imagination.[27] Often they were given the status of marvels and prodigies and placed on display as won-drous performers.[28] Such displays are intrinsic to the legacy and theatrical programs of the modern day freak show, such as the ven-ues that exhibited Tripp. This gambler incarnates his glamorous and deeply historical reputation as a trickster and risk taker. A gambler in a present day casino setting is on display for his wondrous dex-terity at shuffling, dealing, and performing card tricks that fool the eye, in stark contrast with Tripp's mundane and debased "tricks." Both images stage the acts of amputee bodies as miraculous, yet in Witkin's image, the gambler is supernatural, and perhaps his "hands-on" practices make a witty reference to Witkin's own mirac-ulous displays. Witkin's *Gambler* embodies a character known for its voyeuristic appeal within the casino, as Witkin plays upon the disabled body as spectacle. His objectification of such bodies comments on their historical objectification as bodies on display, albeit ambiguously. Witkin's photographs contribute to objectification of bodies (they are neither portraits of individuals nor social documentary images); they tell us little about these people's lives, and he claims his hired actors become depersonalized, still life icons or corporeal symbols of artistic emotions when photographed. They are symbolic bodies made graphically "real" and material by photography, here emphasized as a hybrid of artistic fiction and science that takes such themes to an excessive level. Witkin's images take risks, embodied here by the *Gambler* himself. This amputee takes risks by nature of his gambling role within the frame, as well as by the act of the model taking on this role—posing in the photograph, which is perhaps a form of self-objectification.

The magical qualities of *Gambler*, and Witkin's photographic alchemy, defy scientific and logical explanation. Staged by Witkin as theatrical, amputee bodies seduce and ultimately reject a diagnostic gaze—the causes of impairment for the model in *Gambler* are not revealed in the photograph. Rather, *Gambler* and other amputee subjects deliver embodied performances that solicit the gaze and embodied viewer responses through self-exhibition of their own extraordinariness. The *Gambler* exercises his power to maintain partial invisibility—to withhold from the viewer as the image withholds his personal identity and diagnosis—symbolized by his theatrical mask. The mask signifies that the model is as an actor playing a role. The mask, in another ironic twist on a clinical blocking of the eyes, enables the *Gambler* to return a gaze that is seductively concealed. Again, as a reference to a tarot card, the composition privileges the antiscientific realms of magic, mystery, and the supernormal.

Genealogies of disability often suggest that the medical model, based in Enlightenment values and scientific emphasis, worked to eclipse premodern discourses of anomaly or human curiosities as supernatural. Indeed, the nineteenth century saw the establishment of teratology, the science of monsters, which classified many disabled bodies as monstrous "others," diagnosed them, and attempted to eradicate anomaly from the population. Yet discourses of disability as wondrous, spectacular, even supernatural or divinely heroic continued on in freak shows, special interest media stories, popular culture (largely film), fine art, and daily social values. Witkin began photographing 1970s sideshow performers at Coney Island and elsewhere, such as Melvin Burkhart, whose talents included driving nails up his nose (an act captured in Witkin's portrait: *Melvin Burkhart, Human Oddity* [1985]). Diane Arbus, whose work is the focus of the next chapter, also turned her camera to these sideshows of the 1960s and 1970s. Photographing performers whom many would call the dying breed of freaks, while others would call the next generation, Witkin's and Arbus's photographs document how the freak show has lived on, and often by the choice of contemporary individuals they feature.

Witkin's images bring all these discourses and representations of "abnormality" to the fore, albeit fantastically. His images reveal how different contexts and conventions of representation operate in interpretations of his photographs and judgments on the bodies they display. These discursive connotations are again never "wholly" liberating or derogatory for the social construction of disability, in material culture and everyday life, and certainly not in Witkin's often controversial work. Yet Witkin never claims to present a "whole" and unified work that can be contextualized or contained in one discursive frame. As I have illustrated here with images of dissection and amputation, Witkin's work is unapologetically "unwhole" in specific rejection of notions of "whole" as preferable.

One final example of an amputee in Witkin's frames draws together various discursive fragments and representations of the disabled, specifically amputee body in visual culture. In Witkin's *Abundance* (1997) we see a "human torso" or an amputee woman with no legs and disfigured hands, not as an object of scientific study or a freak attraction, but instead presented as an eroticized sculptural object of beauty, placed on an urn, and crowned with an offering of succulent fruit. The vignette corners of the frame gives the image an antique quality, and further, makes it theatrical rather than medical. The darkened background sets off her white, marblelike skin and the contours of her bare breasts. Witkin presents this amputee as a hybridized, ornamental still life object reminiscent of garden statuary in Rococo design, particularly in the erotic and playful productions of painters Jean-Honoré Fragonard and Antione Watteau. These eighteenth-century artists' decorative, anthropomorphic fountains and urns spew and collect the source of life, in art historical programs (namely, Rococo) that have been gendered female due to their bodily, imaginary, and decorative excesses. *Abundance* again resembles a Neoclassical sculpture and critiques Classical notions of the body as art. *Abundance* is a theatrical performance of an amputee, transplanted from a pejorative notion of undesirable abnormality to a product from the garden of earthly delights.

Witkin's *Abundance* subtracts the amputee from an everyday social realm in which she might be considered, in colloquial terms, deformed or disabled, due to her deviation from norms and the consequential social obstacles that exclude her. Witkin places her on stage and perhaps problematically immobilizes her on an urn. The body is here objectified as an ornamental object—another theatrical prop or metaphorical symbol like the abundant fruit. Yet, in Witkin's tableau her embodied, multidimensional, multireferential, indeed abundant significance overpowers her physical immobilization, as the amputee performs as an allegory of abundance in a context of sensual pleasures and excessive erotic play. She is an aesthetic object tangibly embodied, as the photographic medium again articulates the materiality of her flesh, here overflowing and fecund. Like the urn, Witkin's framing fails to contain this extraordinary body. Fused with the urn, she is posed as a spectacular, hybridized body showcased in a hybridized photograph—one that fuses and confuses the bodily displays of science and art.

## Dismembering Images

Witkin's images are intricately dangerous, yet raise profoundly provocative issues regarding historical representation of disability. What is the status of the disabled body in the context of Witkin's preoccupations with the taboo, the macabre, the confrontational, and the infinitely freakish, as well as in the context of Classical traditions? With art historical references in particular, Witkin engages disabled bodies in dramas of myth, violence, monstrosity, and the supernatural, calling attention to their historical inclusion in such frames, yet simultaneously repeating some of the precarious subtexts that such legacies embody. Witkin's work raises weighty questions about the framing of bodies across genres of visual culture.

The images showcase bodies that exceed conventional frames for representation, as they cross the boundaries between depicting the body as a representational metaphor and the body as flesh. Witkin's models are unashamedly excessive and curious; they are photographically showcased as bodies without legislation, as they cannot be contained within social classifications and norms for bodies, genres of visual culture, or even Witkin's photographic frames. The images create a counter-aesthetic, beyond designations of normal and abnormal; further, they provide a stage for amputee actors to parade their corporealities, unashamedly, and to perform with their fantastical bodies.

One may ask whether Witkin's models benefit at all from self-objectification. Early medical photography often represented low income, immigrant, or otherwise "underprivileged" subjects to convey medicine as improving society. It often solicited models or patients who would place their bodies on public display, like still life objects and the possessions of science, in exchange for medical services.[29] In an intriguing shuffle, Witkin's subjects are models and actors hired for performing crafts that might be already considered forms of exhibitionism. Self-display hereby provides a service and financial, at least, and perhaps professional gain for the subjects. Particularly in the case of sideshow performers, Witkin's actors are already involved in self-display before they meet his camera. One wonders how many opportunities some receive for other working options, whether involving exhibitionism or not, when faced with social ideals for public bodies and accessibility of public spaces. Amputee models, for example, collaborate with Quinn in attempts to reframe the vision of their bodies in society with the legacy of Classical beauty, for more personal gains. Witkin's photography may serve as a venue for certain subjects' employment and public visibility.

Witkin's formal look of early photography performs subversively; he appropriates medical photography's conventions for displaying bodies and redefines the terms of objectification. His antique aesthetic also brings into a contemporary setting the representation of the body circulated by early medical photography, reminding us that the framing of bodies as medical cases is neither fixed in the past nor contained to the realm of photography. In Witkin's world, abnormal individuals, like the actors he hires, continue to confront a history of being medicalized and constructed in opposition to whatever society deems is physically preferable. The normal body today is viewed as improvable through medical "progress," standardized, and regulated through self-disciplinary actions and restrictions (diet and exercise, for examples). The ideal market by popular culture may be approached only through chemical and surgical alteration; aging and disability are to be avoided at all costs. Comparatively, bodies that will forever fail to fit the mold, such as the excessive, unclassifiable, and amputated bodies Witkin features, become exemplary of wrong or abnormal bodies—worthy of pity and scorn. Yet Witkin's camera eroticizes, animates, and aestheticizes them through the camera's eye. They become Classical, immortal beauties.

Much of Witkin's work is disarming, as it solicits and holds the gaze/stare in fascination, humor, and fear. It demands questioning of *why* it is disturbing rather than how. Witkin's work is most often characterized as portraying human violence, tragedy, shame, and ultimately death, but I see much of it remarking on the most fundamental issues of life and vitality: hedonism, exhibitionism, sensuality, desire, eroticism, the body in pain, and the scope of human diversity. Witkin's work challenges cultural assumptions and judgments of bodies, what they do, and what should bring them pleasure. It forces us to confront our greatest fears, anxieties, and inhibitions about our own bodies, our morality, and inevitable mortality. His work asks us to see bodies on display in conventional and unconventional contexts, as it interrogates the interactions of scientific, artistic, and social gazes. Witkin's photographs are visually sumptuous and excessive, dynamic, yet timeless. In these unsettling configurations of the body and arrangements of body parts, Witkin's photographs showcase the inevitable eroticism of the flesh and exhibit how the "abnormal" may be infinitely desirable.[30]

# 4

# Exceeding the Frame

In photographer Diane Arbus's (1923–1971) eccentric portrait suite, a giant bows down to his parents; little people loom large; nudists inhabit family rooms and backyards; sideshow and burlesque characters display tattoos, swallow swords, contort their bodies, and pose on and off the stage; hermaphrodites and transvestites are caught in the costumed acts of everyday life; toddlers throw temper tantrums; unruly children hold hand grenades, smoke cigarettes, or bend over backward for the camera; dancehall contestants freeze in their tracks; overage beauty queens flaunt inappropriate dress; opposites attract and reproduce; garish faces scowl, eyes roll back in heads, and the forlorn look longingly beyond the frames. In short, Arbus captures the idiosyncratic masses masquerading and parading indiscretion. Through intense exchanges of gazes and stares between the subjects, the viewers, and Arbus's camera, desire and alienation crystalize. Everyday and extraordinary people make spectacular spectacles of themselves in these images, enacting everyday life as theatrical, bizarre, and carnivalesque. In Arbus's photographs, every pairing is an odd couple, and individuals of all shapes, sizes, colors, classes, and walks of life become eccentric—indeed, even freakish.

Many view such "freakishness" in the photographs through the lens of Arbus's life. Born to an upper-class Jewish family of New York City store owners, Arbus had a privileged upbringing and esteemed career as a fashion photographer (in collaboration with her husband, photographer Allan Arbus), and yet was always drawn to various offbeat subcultures. For example, she frequented Hubert's Museum in Times Square, a revival sideshow venue, befriending and photographing many of the performers, and she was known to visit venues for display such as Coney Island and local wax museums. Arbus's personal and professional affinity for the freakish has been largely associated with her lifelong bout with depression, self-image as a social outcast, and 1971 suicide, as her freak subjects have been seen as surrogate self portraits or metaphors for Arbus's own alienation, fragmentation, and uncertainty about her body.[1] These accusations have been waged often to explain Arbus's so-called exploitation of disabled people as pitiful and tragic outcasts. Therefore, Arbus's artistic reputation and biography, in direct association with her choice of subjects, have established her as a freak. These assumptions restrictively frame Arbus's portraits, as well as the subjects she showcases, and perhaps reveal more about the viewer than the body on display.

Arbus's photographic "body aesthetic" (her formal framing of the body) was intentional. Arbus may be said to caricature all of her subjects, disabled and nondisabled, by exaggerating their most eccentric or idiosyncratic qualities. In these ways, the images construct everyday life as excessive through strategic, photographic staging and intentional image manipulation. From the 1960s onward, Arbus strategically employed a twin lens Rollieflex camera for its square-frame format, intense details, and exaggerated distortion of image edges. She is also known for her hand-printing techniques, often producing articulated borders and frames around her images. Arbus continued to produce commercial and fashion photographs throughout life.[2] Yet, in sharp contrast with the fashion photographs of her contemporaries, and some say in intentional opposition to them, Arbus's "freak" photographs have a distinct amateur quality. This graininess is characteristic of a 1960s and 1970s street photography, which turned away from earlier formalist trends of art photography and incorporated the ethnographic traditions of documentary. This work also questioned how photography made a subject into art. Making the disabled body into art and spectacle, Arbus indeed frames the dubious roles of disability in visual representation.

The strongest assaults on Arbus's photography target the certain kinds of people she features, including disabled people, and what the viewer assumes about them through Arbus's frames. Reactions to Arbus's work seem polarized as some are seduced to partake in her pleasure of looking, specifically at people who stand out in a crowd,[3] while others, unable to escape similar temptation in spite of themselves, criticize the pictures as exploitative, disturbing, and pessimistic.[4] For example, art critic Judith Goldman (1974) writes, "Her subjects were people on the edges—the physically malformed—dwarfs, midgets, giants, twins, and transvestites with sideshow relationships to society, and physically normal people, whose edge was a fact of their social class and whose condition, like the malformed, was loneliness and the psychological despair of boredom."[5] Like Goldman, many recognize Arbus's almost extrasensory peripheral vision—her magnetic attraction to the peripheries or margins of mainstream society. Arbus is often said to show, indeed hyperbolize and glorify, that which is not normally seen—what, or who, goes unnoticed by the assumed "normal" viewer;[6] whereas others recognize that her subjects capture attention precisely because they are a striking visible disturbance in artistic and social fields of "normal" human subjects.[7] Poignantly, the images frame the viewer in their act of staring.

Arbus's work traffics in the dynamics of the gaze/stare. Disability studies scholar and photographer David Hevey (1992) has charged Arbus specifically with "enfreakment," arguing that Arbus's images problematically frame disabled people as freaks, outcasts, and derogatorily abnormal "others."[8] In opposition, I argue these labels are more derogatory and oppressive than the images themselves, for they foreclose the possibility of seeing more dimensions. Goldman writes further, "Though trained not to admit it, we are fascinated by the aberrant, the violent, and the perverse. When we are assured no one's watching, we stare at cripples and auto wrecks."[9] This quote stands out to me for several reasons that lead into visual analysis of images:

1. What exactly is the association between so-called cripples, and auto wrecks as spectacles—as awesome objects of a questioning, captivating, and fearful gaze?
2. What are the implications of looking without being seen and without anyone looking back at you?
3. Does photography somehow offer an anonymous, disembodied gaze for the viewer versus other spectacle venues, particularly live ones?

I would argue no, particularly in the case of Arbus's photography, for many of her images exclude the possibility of looking without being seen and looking at oneself. If nothing else might be agreed upon in judgments of her work, it defies disinterest—it solicits and manipulates the embodied, multidirectional and multidimensional gazes of the photographer, the viewer, and disabled subjects.

In this chapter, I will focus on three Arbus photographs that feature subjects engaged in distinct sets of dynamic gazes. My chosen examples embody layered scenarios of gazing and staring and disruptively exceed the frames of conventional visual representations of disabled bodies. I will place Arbus's work in broader contexts of visual culture through formal and discursive comparisons to images from art history, early medical photography and other medical displays, the American freak show of the nineteenth and early twentieth century, and more recent popular culture. Referencing multiple traditions of portraiture particularly, Arbus makes multireferential portraits of her disabled subjects that reveal how certain socially conspicuous individuals indeed combat a history of being portrayed as medical specimens, freaks, and creatures of myth. Arbus's images exaggerate, overlap, and combine multiple visual genres, complicating and enriching her work's interpretive potentials. Arbus's photographs add to the history of disabled bodies on display and under scrutiny of the gaze in cultural representation and everyday life, yet self-consciously. Rather than wholly defending or castigating Arbus's portrayal of disability, I perhaps do some of both and expose the many oppositions and contradictions operating within their frames, which gives the images and their subjects more dimensions. In the following sections, I will reframe Arbus's so-called freakish or disabled subjects as performative agents through alternative readings of their portraits.

### Larger than Life

In 1970 the petite Arbus transported her weighty Rollieflex camera to the home of Eddie Carmel and his parents. Carmel, at thirty-four years of age, 8 feet tall, and 300 pounds, had been born with acromegaly, a tumor on the pituitary gland that produced excess of growth hormones and made his lips, jaw, hands, and feet swell.[10] From birth, Carmel never ceased expanding. He had learned early in life that his excessive body was the bane of his existence, his greatest asset, and in the eyes of most normal people, his defining characteristic, and he pursued a career in show business. Carmel tried stand up comedy and voice-overs, recorded the song "The Good Monster," played a bit part in the film "The Brain that Wouldn't Die" (1963), made circus and sideshow appearances, and starred in advertising. His work in voice acting may suggest he desired fame outside of voyeuristic draw to his body; nevertheless, he became a recognizable local celebrity and established freak. Eventually, Carmel's body outgrew his fame and overcame him; he died two years after Arbus photographed him. Arbus's portrait serves as a memorial to Carmel and was the inspiration for the biographical radio program, now available on compact disc, researched and narrated by one of his cousins.[11]

Arbus shot a series of images of Carmel and his parents; the one developed into *Jewish Giant at Home with His Parents in the Bronx, NY* (1970) employs a composition and developing process that exaggerates Carmel's largess. This image features Carmel in the center of a working-class family's living room leaning on one cane, towering over, and gazing down at his two comparatively miniature parents, who stare back up at him with facial expressions of awe, amazement, and perhaps a bit of fear. The grainy quality of Arbus's technique and the detail captured by her camera emphasize this nonidealistic atmosphere in an amateur style family photo. The compositional arrangement and exchange of gazes may be interpreted as an ominous family album snapshot of parents confronting the monster they have created. The blurred and shadowed edges emphasized by the Rollieflex camera implicate viewers in peeping at the spectacle of Carmel's body, as if placing their faces against cupped hands and gazing through a neighbor's window. Or perhaps the viewer is stationed in the foregrounded armchair, appearing only partially in the frame, and placed at eye level with Carmel's massive legs. The viewer is uncomfortably present in this private scene and partly transgresses the frame, in interplays between spectacle and spectator. This experience might be quite different from looking at Carmel on stage, in a crowd of separated audience members. The photography displays how Carmel is inevitably subject to a social stare. He stands out by standing head and shoulders above others and does not fit in, even in his own home and context of his family. Contrary to the laws of science, two like individuals have reproduced an offspring with fantastical physical difference.

A desire to view the photograph—to stare at Carmel—engages the association of looking at "cripples" and auto wrecks. Carmel, common to many of his stature or condition, was indeed impaired by his excessive and relentless physical growth—the cane in the image eventually became two and then a wheelchair, followed by Carmel's death. Yet Carmel is also "crippled," or "disabled," in the photograph by definition of disability as a socially constructed, oppressed identity; he is made into an abnormal "other" by environments, architectures, and social attitudes that exclude and reject him, seen here in the form of his living room and the disconcerted family with whom he shares it. Freak show performer and biographer of freaks, Daniel P. Mannix (1969) points also to the financial burdens that disable individuals with abnormal bodies, like Carmel, due to their need for specialized clothing, shoes, personal items, vehicles, environmental adaptations, and other provisions.[12] The spectacular image perhaps capitalizes on Carmel's tragedies—Carmel frequently lamented his status as social outcast, far more than complaining of his physical aches and pains[13]—similarly to staring at an auto wreck. However, Arbus's image in this way also incriminates the viewer in Carmel's personal pain, as their stares contribute to his freak status. Many narrate this image as a tragic tale of a gentle giant. However, Arbus's photographic composition, emphasizing graphically Carmel's physical oppression, tells additional stories, for Carmel's body literally and figuratively exceeds the frame.

Arbus's framing of Carmel exceeds conventional photographic genres for viewing bodies, particularly spectacular ones like Carmel's, on visual display. Literary theorist Rachel Adams (2001) has compared Arbus's images with nineteenth and early-twentieth-century cartes de visites, widely popular, postcard-sized, collectible portrait photographs that marketed eccentric freak show performers as celebrities.[14] A carte by Charles Eisenmann of the *Texas Giant Brothers* (c. 1880) features a trio of tall brothers in distinguished period suits, lined up and flanked by two compositional props—a book on a table ledge at the left side of the photograph and a sculpted wood banister pot on the right. Below the image each "giant's" age and height is displayed, ranging from 7 feet to 8 feet tall. Arbus's style echoes many of the formal qualities of early freak photography: grainy quality; strongly contrasting blacks and whites; and frontally lit, central framing of the full body.[15] Freak shows share with Arbus's work a combining and overlapping of genres for displaying spectacular bodies.

Adams relates Arbus's characteristic form to clinical elements of freak show cartes de visites, drawn from the genre of diagnostic medical photography. Conventional clinical photographs, with their diagnostic texts, offered medical legitimacy to extraordinary spectacle anomalies of the freak show. The bodily remains of individuals exhibited as freaks often became medical displays after they died, as was commonly the case with giants. Photographer Rosamund Purcell has illustrated and narrated books on visual collections, medical displays, and exhibits of human curiosities and anomalies. In *Special Cases: Natural Anomalies and Historical Monsters*, based on a Getty exhibit she curated, Purcell includes a photograph of the skeleton of a 7 feet 6 inches man who died in his early twenties in late nineteenth century, displayed in the Mütter Museum in Philadelphia, Pennsylvania.[16] In the appropriate conventions of clinical photographs, Purcell frames the skeleton in profile to highlight the unique curvature of his spine, a consequence of his tall stature that caused impairments. Arbus's image of Carmel likewise utilizes this posture to accentuate his spectacular body and his impairments.

In *Jewish Giant*, we are presented with a full body, profile view of Carmel, characteristic of freak show and medical photography. Albeit hunched over, Carmel's magnificent stature is further exaggerated by the pairing with his noticeably dwarfed parents, in a freakish dualism of the miniature and the gigantic. An example of this freak show motif is a black and white publicity photograph of *Jack Earle, Giant Poet*,[17] which features a giant performer photographed at pelvic level to emphasize his height, and in particular, the length of his limbs. In the space between his treelike, spread legs stands an ambiguous man/child little person wearing a tie, whose smallness accentuates the massive body that poses above him. The image appears humorous in its irony of sizes. Such offsets of opposites are characteristic pairings seen in freak show venues and photographs. Carmel was a known freak performer, yet little information is offered in Arbus's image about his condition, or what caused his so-called monstrous freakishness, thus rejecting a medical, diagnostic gaze. He is not posed in a characteristic clinical composition (most often minimal or absent in background) nor freak show carte setting, which were conventional studio settings with a few highly iconic props and scaled environments. Arbus's is not a formal studio portrait—the image places Carmel in his home environment, indication of his social and economic identity. Arbus's images often highlight bodies in personalized, even idiosyncratic settings, yet less strategically staged than studio portraits.[18] Carmel is "at home," rather than featured in a freak show venue or carte de visite, medical, documentary, or anthropological image of an "exotic"—all forms that conventionally motivate, justify, and mediate a viewer's gaze.

Arbus's work is said to either "enfreak" (construct subjects as freaks and make them abnormal) or "normalize" them through private viewings, adding another layer of confusing oppositions to the images. Arbus produces ambiguous pairings of the opposites normal/abnormal. Arbus chose this image for public display, rather than a number of others from her contact sheet, which show the family embracing, smiling, and posing frontally for the camera, as typical for a family photo. He is enfreaked—his largess exaggerated—in the photograph compared with the others, and at the same time normalized, or "at home." In this final image, Carmel does not offer the viewer a compliant returned gaze, as perhaps one would if engaged in freakish self-display, and instead turns his gaze to his parents, withholding knowledge from the viewer as to why they should be so entranced by staring at him and what benefit or information they receive from it. He refuses to acknowledge the viewer in his performance, perhaps transforming staged spectating into unsanctioned staring or peeping.

## Giant Metaphors

Arbus's gaze directs, but not does limit the viewer's gaze at Carmel in the photograph. Shortly before taking this photograph, Arbus wrote in a postcard, "One more thing, perhaps too exotic . . . I know a Jewish giant who lives in Washington Heights or the Bronx with his little parents. He is tragic with a curious bitter somewhat stupid wit. The parents are orthodox and repressive and classic and disprove of this carnival career . . . Once many years ago I photographed them but I don't know where it is . . . They are a truly metaphorical family . . . (sic)."[19] For Arbus, Carmel's family was a metaphor, but for what?: her own conservative Jewish family and feelings of being a black sheep or freak?, or for an "average" American family, one in which familial relationships specifically and human relationships in general eclipse human differences? Arbus had a fascination with family groupings at this time, and perhaps in this context, the Carmel family points to the inevitable freakishness of family relations, relating to Arbus's tendency to portray the freakishness of everyday life in her suite of eccentric subjects. Perhaps the Carmel family, dynamically staged in the photograph, represents human relationships in general—always eccentric in pairings. Or perhaps Arbus recognizes the metaphors conventionally associated with such extraordinary embodiments such as Carmel's. The image is not titled with Carmel's name to suggest that it is a particularized portrait. Rather, he is presented as the "Jewish Giant" in an iconic epithet, or like *Texas Giant Brothers*, a freak show stage name, which often hyperbolized and recycled markers of bodily configuration, race, or regional origin across a succession of actors.

The monstrosity or freakishness of Carmel constructed in Arbus's photograph engages a much longer history of such spectacular bodies on display, and particularly the cultural mythologies surrounding giants. Bakhtin (1968) describes the giant as a metaphoric embodiment of cosmic forces; thus giants are imagined in myth and lore as means for average sized humans to confront and conceptualize unexplained phenomena.[20] Freak shows capitalized on this association, as in the example of the "Chinese Giant," Chang Yu Sang, who appeared at various sideshow venues in the nineteenth and early twentieth century. Born in Peking in 1847, Sang was over 8 feet tall and embodied Chinese mythological and cosmological beliefs that giants were present in rocks. Extending beyond cultures that believe in animated nature, associations of giants with natural environments, particularly mountains, is common in fiction, freak personas, and various forms of display, as giants become worthy of natural history. Leslie Fiedler's extensive study of freak show characters points to the number of civilizations that, according to origin myths, arose from a society's defeat of giants (Greeks, Hebrew, Norse),[21] as literature often features giants as a race of people, not singular "freaks."

Depictions of giants as a race raise additional, specifically racist, discourses to Arbus's portrait of Carmel as a "Jewish Giant." Sander Gilman (1978) analyzes the multiple discursive modes of anti-Semitism operating in visual culture, represented in depictions of particular body parts and behaviors and pejorative significations constructed around them.[22] A major theme Gilman pursues is the nose, which is articulated and best exaggerated by the convention of profile shots—a clinical and schematic convention employed and subverted by Arbus. Gilman argues that visions of the nose as a racially identifying characteristic signify a range of disparaging social stereotypes of Jews. Significantly, such representations cross popular, artistic, and clinical images in their conventions for depicting the Jewish body, which reveals these genres as interconnected and mutually contributing to ideological myths. In relation, Arbus's portrait of a "Jewish Giant" engages multiple depictions of the Jewish, as well as the Giant body. The social stigma articulated by Arbus's "Jewish Giant" (Carmel) frames contemporary forms of racism (which she experienced as a Jewish woman in postwar American society) and stems from a longer history of cultural myths.

Giants have been cast in myths surrounding "other" lands and peoples historically, for examples in the many tales of giants in Western travel narratives of foreign, exotic lands. Like myths, freak shows present ethnic giants, as in the example of the Chinese Giant, as stock characters, exploiting cultural associations of giants with place or race. The "Irish Giant" was Charles Byrne, whose bones are now in the Royal College of Surgeons of London on medical display, and the role was later played by Patrick O'Brien. Additional examples of performers include Anna H. Swann, the "Nova Scotia Giantess"; Angus McAskill, the "Scottish Giant," featured in Barnum's American Museum; and the "Icelandic Giant," a character played by Johann K. Peterson, who came to the United States in 1948, appeared in many sideshows, and progressed to a very profitable, one-man show, in which he wore Viking costume, large headdress to emphasize his size, and long beard. These actors performed as cultural/historical characters tied to their ethnic heritage and wore stereotypical, fictional costumes. In these examples and many others, freak show giants come from cultures that have rich traditions of myths and legends, and these origins are exaggerated in their presentations. As racial/cultural "others" to an American audience, they were enfreaked in size and ethnicity, whereas in other contexts (among others physically and culturally like them), they were normal. Scholars have pointed out that ancient writings suggest humans were closer in height to what we consider giants today and gradually degenerated.[23] Normal and abnormal size varies over time and differs by context.

Individuals of extreme stature combat a formidable history of fictional characters that typecast them, many of which loom in *Jewish Giant*. From Dante's inclusion of giants in Hell, to Cyclops, to Titan, to painter Francisco de Goya's mythological *Colossus* (1808–1812) (a painting of a massive male body from the waist up, emerging from the clouds and threateningly towering over a small village in the bottom half of the painting), to the antagonist of Jack and the Beanstalk, giants are cannibalistic, tyrannical, and feared—constructed as monstrous, like Carmel, and offset by the vulnerable (often, in fiction, little people). Often likened to perhaps the most infamous Jewish giant of all, Goliath, Carmel becomes the subject of a history painting, an allegorical figure like Goya's *Saturn Devouring His Children* (1821–1823) (a horrific image of the mythical giant with bulging eyes and with blood dripping from his jaws as he eats a miniature being, his own child, from his hands). Saturn literally and figuratively consumes his vulnerable family members in an overpowering gaze—perhaps akin to Carmel's? Such a comparison makes Carmel a monster.

Yet in other contexts, giants have different personas. In addition to cosmological embodiments, giants also represent, according to Bakhtin, wealth and abundance through excessive consumption, for which they were often featured at celebratory feasts. The fictional giants Gargantua and Pantagruel in Rabelais text, from which Bakhtin derives his metaphors and theories, are consuming and hedonistic, metaphors for the celebration of life through excess and bodily pleasure, rather than threatening or horrific. As travelers, their girth enables them to consume the wealth of Renaissance knowledge and the fruits of the world.[24] In present day contexts, giants are prized, such as athletes who, like Carmel, reach celebrity status through embodied performances. In addition to numerous basketball players, a poignant, freakish example is the subcultural phenomena, Andre the Giant, who performed as a film actor after his career in the somewhat burlesque theater, or arena, of professional wrestling. Featured in a publicity photo (c. 1980s), which recycles the pairing of opposites found in myths, fairy tales, and freak shows, Andre, again shot at waist level to enhance his largess, supports a gaggle of admiring female fans on his massive shoulders.

Across a suite of often contradictory historical images, societies assess and assign labels to bodies such as "abnormal" or "freakish" according only to frameworks of presentation. Despite that he is an actor, Carmel, of the "Jewish Giant" cannot be typecast due to his body; quite the contrary, for Arbus's "Jewish Giant" embodies infinite historical roles and symbolic connotations. The portrait of Carmel thus exceeds the frames and contexts of visual representation, displaying Carmel in an image repertoire of historical giants and suggesting his status in 1970 as always already on display, even "at home." The image surpasses genres of fictional representation, as Arbus highlights some of Carmel's "larger than life" embodied experiences; for example, posed with his cane, Carmel displays impairments and mortal complications common among individuals with such large stature, contradicting the mythological persona of the giant as a beast of formidable strength. Arbus's image is appropriately excessive and embodies contradiction—Carmel's body is confined to her frame as he hunches over, yet his potential power to exceed the frames is overwhelming to the viewer, while he turns away from them, perhaps enacting invisibility from full exploitation.

### Size Matters

In Arbus's *Mexican Dwarf (a.k.a Cha Cha) in His Hotel Room* (1970), a dwarf, or little person, consumes the frame. His body is aggrandized in a freak show fashion by Arbus's image (again like a freak show carte de visite in certain formal qualities). Cha Cha, like Carmel, was a self-displayed and thus self-proclaimed freak, which drew Arbus to him. He becomes part of a long history of little people on display in Western culture. In addition to becoming supernatural and medical monsters, like giants, little people were uniquely kept at royal courts as prodigies, jesters, comic fools and clowns, and the caretakers and entertainers of royal children. These little people performed their amusements before the family and guests, portrait artists (most popularly Diego Velásquez), and before society at large in private quarters ("at home") and in public fairs, festivals, celebrations, and other spectacles. In the genre of art historical portraiture, dwarfs are included iconographically as miniature offsets to reinforce the authority, austerity, and power of an often elaborately costumed king or queen, as exemplified in Alonso Sánchez Coello's sixteenth century painting *Magdelena Ruíz with Doña Isabel, Clara Eugenía and Monkey* (here also with a monkey), or often paired with other symbolic subjugates like dogs and particularly female children. A major example of this convention is Diego Velásquez's canonical *Las Meniñas* (1656), a portrait of the Spanish royal family that ironically foregrounds the traditionally disempowered—the princess or *infanta* Margarita, her attendant female servants, two court dwarfs, and the loyal pet dog, lying down to accentuate his submission.

About two centuries later, the American freak show employed many little people to perform. In one example, Lucia Zarate, "the smallest woman" (1880) is featured center stage and centrally framed in a photograph from the Dr. Stanley Burns' archive of clinical photography.[25] This image crosses the genres of medicine and the popular entertainment, as was characteristic of the medical/fantastical presentations of the freak show. Freak show little people were often staged alongside amiable giants, as mentioned earlier, to exaggerate their caricatured smallness. To enhance the miniature body, little people were alternatively assigned larger than life personas and names, in what Robert Bogdan has termed an aggrandized mode of presentation,[26] a pairing of opposites. This method exploited historical and iconographic connections between little people and ironic parody. The most famous was P. T. Barnum's "General Tom Thumb," born Charles. S. Stratton. Tom Thumb (as he was constructed through his public performances, marketing materials, and souvenir photographic portraits) embodied long traditions of mythological, literary, and historical little bodies on display, particularly as performers. Arbus's photograph of Cha Cha functions similarly by physically aggrandizing, exaggerating, and making him a metaphor as the nonparticularized "Mexican Dwarf," yet with significant twists on convention.

A comparison of Arbus's portrait of a dwarf with two freak show cartes de visites, a characteristic wedding shot of Charles Stratton and his wife, Lavinia Warren (who shared a popular public spectacle wedding orchestrated by notorious showman P. T. Barnum in 1963, and whose wedding portrait became the most profitable carte de visites of all time) and Eisenmann's carte of Admiral Dot (c. 1881), proves illuminating. They share strong frontal lighting, an Arbus trademark, and similar staging of props to characterize the little people and their shared bodily, performative magnificence. The carte of Stratton and his wife pairs them as sentimentalized miniatures in miniature costumes and presents them as children, set to scale by a mantelpiece. They are infantilized as in many historical royal portraits, although their "owner" (here Barnum versus a king) is absent in the photograph, according to conventions specific to early portrait photography. Cartes de visite images often drew attention to the performer's bodies, charming and entertaining public appeal (sometimes including instruments and props for musical numbers or comic impressions), and celebrity personas, rather than their status as freaks. Admiral Dot is featured in top hat holding a baton against an arched doorway with Corinthian columns, a stage setting used repeatedly by Eisenmann to accentuate "little" subjects' statures. In Arbus's image, Cha Cha's body fills the frame in a stylistically distinctive square format with darkened, blurred edges created by the Rollieflex, which perhaps condenses and exaggerates his physical smallness. These formal techniques place the image in the traditions of depicting dwarf bodies as caricatures and subjects of parody.

Extending beyond Arbus's photography, fine art enters in these discourses on and representations of little people. Velásquez's painting of a dwarf kept at the Spanish court, *The Dwarf Sebastian de Morra* (c. 1645), like Arbus's photograph, frames and aggrandizes (in a close-up perspective) the full body of its subject in historical costume, here seated with his hands curled under suggesting that he may have physical impairments. His ambivalent return gaze, as compared with Cha Cha's, seems reluctant, almost vacant, or stereotypically idiotic. Mannix (1999) states that historically, by being or *behaving* idiotic, court dwarfs were able to speak freely, criticize, and mock authority,[27] such that performative gestures, which manipulated their subordinate and comic reputations, gained little people the statuses of royal sidekicks and prodigies. Velásquez's painting suggests the privileged status of Sebastian de Morra at court, for it is a conventional, individual portrait, perhaps commissioned, rather than a composition that presents a dwarf as a domesticated offset to reinforce royal power. The portrait, like Arbus's of Cha Cha, showcases and strongly lights the body, in what perhaps could be a clinical, full body format found in medical/freak show images like the one of Lucia Zarate. Indeed, early portrait photography based its compositional techniques on painting. This centered perspective of the photography accentuates Cha Cha's abnormality, similar to Sebastian de Morra's. All of these compositions, although belonging in different sociohistorical contexts, similarly frame the abnormal "little" body, albeit according to contextually specific conventions.

Compositional props in these portraits function to cross and confuse such contexts for viewing an abnormal body. Normal or conventional portraits may have included a chair, whereas Sebastian de Morra is seated in the floor. Is this because he cannot stand? Arbus's Mexican Dwarf is seated also unconventionally, but here, on a bed suggestively. Unlike Arbus's photograph, Velásquez's painting places the dwarf against a voided, chiaroscuro backdrop, characteristic of period portraiture. However, due to the abnormal subject this technique may be read in other contexts as a clinical or natural history style, which excludes surrounding props that might identify him as an individual social subject. This technique could work to represent di Morra as a generic or stock character—an often comic, performative persona whose function or popular draw for the audience could be played by successive actors, as was often the case in freak shows—rather than an individual in a portrait. Conversely, Arbus's image includes props, in photographic portrait convention, to hint at a narrative surrounding Cha Cha as a historical subject and perhaps at his personality. Such inclusion of props places Arbus's photograph again in conversation with early photography, specifically the freak show carte, a form that exploited this convention to construct the popular personas of little people.

The props in *Mexican Dwarf*, like those in freak show cartes de visites, tell stories about the centered man, and here specifically occupy the margins of the image as if to suggest their deceptive staging within the frame. These marginal props are framing devices that help define the central image. They are significantly ambiguous. We cannot help but take notice of the dwarf man's body dominating the photograph, as would likely be the case beyond the frames public display (in everyday life, for little people stand out as they stand up in a "normal" crowd), yet we also notice the hat that could place him fashionably in specific sociohistorical context, as well as indicate his social status. And what of the half-empty bottle of liquor, a potential phallic symbol or marker of masculine or deviant behaviors, on the tabletop beside him, half evading the frame? Is he tragically drowning his sorrows for his own freakishness or celebrating his body, or perhaps he is on vacation in this hotel? Is he preparing for a visitor? In relation, what is the significance of the bath towel pulled up to cover the suggested nakedness below his revealed torso: did he just get out of the shower? And what is one to make of the ambiguous human appendage peeking out from his shroud, strategically shadowed in the off-centered foreground? These and other questions about Cha Cha circulate the frame.

Arbus's portrait opens endless interpretive potentials for viewing this body. Hevey (1997), a formidable critic of Arbus's and other nondisabled photographer's "enfreakment" of disabled people, recognizes that this small dwarf foot is a not only an iconographic phallus, but may be visually misrecognized *as* a corporeal, miniature penis. Hevey uses this as evidence of Arbus's so-called negative depictions and exploitations of disabled bodies, yet fails to unpack the layers of possible implications of Arbus's constructed image of a sexualized little person. As well known from fairy tales like "Snow White and the Seven Dwarfs," male dwarfs are asexually innocent and childlike, or in the case of "Rumplestiltskin," childishly mischievous, and in some versions of the story, hypersexual and immature, like horny adolescents. Contrary to sentimentalizing, infantilizing, and parodying traditions, Arbus presents a virile Man, albeit gender hybridized due to his positioning as a conventionally feminine, sexualized object of an erotic gaze. He is "at home" in his body and its powerful allure—perhaps in command of his sexual display. Similarly, the 2003 film *The Station Agent* (Thomas McCarthy, dir.) presents a little person protagonist, Finbar McBride (played by Peter Dinklage) as an agent—a narrative hero and the object of an erotic gaze, as well as the victim of social stigma. The film progressively places a little person actor in a role that is both conventional for an average size, attractive leading man and specific to the lived experiences of people with small stature. In *Mexican Dwarf*, the public freak spectacle is made private (in his hotel—an already provocative setting) and eroticized, as Arbus's image traffics between canonical art portraiture, documentary photography, and pornography.²⁸ Hevey remarks on the lore that Arbus was in fact sexually involved with this freak, suggesting that what many viewers find disturbing about the image is the relationship between the viewer's perspective and the subject's body. Arbus first photographed Cha Cha in 1963, seven years before this image was produced, and they kept in touch between shooting sessions and until Arbus's death, as was common for Arbus with many of her subjects. She prided herself on her relationships with her subjects, a biographical fact that may be reproduced in her photographic framing of them, and that some see as exploitative, although others view as an attribute to the establishment of her popularity.

The notion that an image articulates the photographer/subject relational dynamics may be reinforced by comparing *Mexican Dwarf* with contemporary Chicago painter Riva Lehrer's 1999 portrait (*Tekki Lomnicki*) of theater actor and performance artist, little person Tekki Lomnicki (Figure 4.1). The painter and her performing subject share agendas for disability rights, pride, and freedom of expression of and with the body through the arts. Both ally with disability studies—one a woman with spina bifida and the other a little woman who uses canes. Their friendship pervades the image, as it features a close-up of Lomnicki's full body similar to Arbus's portrait of Cha Cha, emphasizing her shorter than average, compacted and striking form. The performer smiles broadly and suggestively and stands tall, stabilizing herself with one crutch, while the other has been allowed to fall, or perhaps is cast off, angled in the shallow perspective of the foreground. Dressed (or undressed) in a suggestive white slip and yet to be costumed, Lomnicki is viewed here behind the scenes of her staged performances, performing in a private setting before her colleague. Arbus likewise features many performers behind the scenes in her portrait photograph. This painting blends sentimentalization with seduction, and the up-close-and-personal viewing level creates a relationship between the subject and the viewer, like *Mexican Dwarf*. In Arbus's image, as Cha Cha's body spills over the frame, his hat and foot visually escaping it, an intimacy and sense of touch invades the separation between spectator and spectacle, dismantling the narrative of a one-directional and exploitative gaze.

**Figure 4.1**    Riva Lehrer, *Tekki Lomnicki* (1999)

### Blowing up the Negatives

Little people disrupt the conventional differentiations between "normal" versus "abnormal" bodies. In their own contexts and accommodating, scaled environments, little people are normal, as in the example of giants as a race of beings. Arbus was broadly interested in multiple "miniature" societies like the Hubert's Museum, which existed on the margins of the mainstream and operated by their own rules, norms, and standards for appearance and decorum; examples are nudist camps, freak shows, twin conventions, dancehall contests, annual picnics for the Federation of the Handicapped,[29] institutions for the developmentally disabled, and others. Arbus would "stand out" in these environments, like Gulliver in the land of Lilliputians, perhaps as an interloper, although she often wrote with joy about being embraced by such communities, made to feel "at home," or normal, and felt comfortable participating in the alternative, often carnivalesque lifestyles. For example, one of Arbus's images of people in nudist colonies, *Retired Man and His Wife at Home in a Nudist Camp One Morning* (1963), is a black and white photograph of a naked man and woman posed casually in their living room, quite comfortable and "at home" in their display of nudity. This scene would be unremarkable if they were clothed. Many of Arbus's nudist subjects were photographed while she was in the buff (naked), thus the power dynamics of the gaze were destabilized, at least off the page. This relationship could make the subjects more comfortable and "at home," as in this image of the couple's living room, as they pose for the camera. If nudity/nakedness *always* means vulnerability to an objectifying gaze, what are the implications when the photographer is unclothed, or otherwise sharing the same status or position as the subject?

Does the viewer of Arbus's photograph feel a part of these subcultural communities or excluded from them, like a freak? *Mexican Dwarf* and many other images were shot with Arbus's chosen twin lens Rollieflex, a camera type specifically held at waist level. This camera angle, which Arbus used in numerous portraits, enhances the intimacy between subject and spectator. It also dwarfs all the subjects it frames, including the average sized, such that *Mexican Dwarf* is not necessarily constructed as "abnormal" in the context of Arbus's oeuvres, although the camera angle functions distinctively in this photograph. She photographed Cha Cha at the height at which dwarfs stand, enacting a kind of identifying perspective (as if Arbus were *like him*—a dwarf).

Contemporary photographer Ricardo Gil's images present such a dwarfed viewpoint and are similar to Arbus's as a family album series. A little person, Gil photographs his wife and daughter, both

**Figure 4.2**   Ricardo Gil, *Johann's Kiss* (1999)

little people, from the perspectives at which he views them—literally, in terms of his height, and figuratively, as intimate close-ups that establish affectionate, familial relationships between the subject and the camera's gaze. In *Johann's Kiss* (1999), Gil features his smiling wife centered in the frame, embraced by an average-sized, kneeling man, whose head is cropped at the top of the image (Figure 4.2). Figures in the background are cut off at mid torso; however, this is not the mistake of an amateur. Here, normal size people don't fit in the little woman's privileged, compositional space.

A similar, lower-than-average point of view functions in *Mexican Dwarf*. The viewer is not only dwarfed or "enfreaked" through this perspective, but put at eye level with the Mexican dwarf and entranced and entrapped by his returned stare. This would not be as prominent if Arbus had chosen one of the other images of Cha Cha from her contact sheet, many of which dwarf him in the middle of a larger frame of the room, often playfully lounging on the bed in his casual clothing; these alternative images contextualize Cha Cha as miniature compared to his normal scaled environment, like the carte de visites of Tom Thumb and Admiral Dot, and in many of these alternative views, Cha Cha appears childlike. Arbus chose a more aggrandizing image, soliciting viewers to stare at the full glory of his body and its possible historical and mythical implications. Are his body and his identity as a "Mexican Dwarf" enfreaked or normalized? Must he be *either* a freak *or* normal? The image crosses these conventionalized opposites. The designation as Mexican may make Cha Cha exotic, further eroticized, according to conventional representation, as well as hint at his social status in 1970 New York City as a self-displayed freak and actor. Yet, combined with designation of his stature, Arbus's title points out that dwarfism is transracial. He shares with all humanity a layered identity and background. He is subject to transhistorical and contextually specific oppression. Like everyone, he is always already a freak *and* normal, considering that only context, rather than embodiment, defines each.

## Documenting Difference

Arbus's portrait suite serves as a kind of archive of eccentrics. Her interest in offbeat types places her work in a history of other ethnographic surveys performed with the camera, such as that of German documentary photographer August Sander. Sander's obsessive photographic cataloguing of social types, including disabled people (in *Blind man* [1930] and *Cretin* [1924]) and subcultural and offbeat groups, may be compared to Arbus's mode of work, and a comparison of his portraits to Arbus's illuminates her unique, hybrid style. Sander, for example, created a scientific (so-called objective) archive for assessing and categorizing the status and worth of individuals, which contributed to establishing a social code and order,[30] as he photographed individuals from all professions, classes, and walks of life, including those involved in sideshow venues. Yet despite their scientific attempt at objectivity, like Arbus's portraits, they have a personal quality. For examples, Sander's *Circus Workers*, (1926–1932) and *Group of Circus People*, (1926) go behind the scenes of circus venues, featuring laborers and performers on a break between acts. As part of Sander's black and white photographic series and documentary project, these images serve as evidence of the flavors of early twentieth-century German life and nostalgia for historical entertainment, particularly subcultural forms.

Arbus's images compare and contrast thematically with Sander's. On the occasion of the 1965 at the closing of the Hubert's Museum, the regretful and disappointed Arbus shot a group portrait of its cast, an image titled *Hubert's Obituary* that she tried unsuccessfully to publish.[31] This image memorializes a history of bodily display and the losses of beloved spectacles. Arbus was inspired by Sander's work, and her nostalgic image of the cast of Hubert's Museum visually resembles Sanders' group portraits of *Circus Workers*, yet here they are costumed as performers in their group portrait, rather than laborers, and are intimate in their poses, showing group camaraderie. Hubert's museum was a miniature or subcultural society with its own rules, norms, values, and standards for bodies, as well as its own sanctioning of embodied pleasure.[32] Here, Arbus was a "regular." She photographed one member of this group multiple times (in 1960 and 1963) whom she had especially befriended in her years as a welcomed spectator, the "Russian Midget," Andrew Ratoucheff. He had been a cast member in Todd Browning cult classic *Freaks* (1932), a film which inspired Arbus.[33] Ratoucheff was popular at the Hubert's museum for his impressions of Marilyn Monroe and Maurice Chevalier, as well as his other of personas, such as "Andy Potato Chips," all of which utilized cultural associations of little people with parody and comedy. Arbus's 1963 photograph of Ratoucheff (*Russian Midget Friends in a Living Room on 100th St., NYC* [1963]), however, does not echo a publicity or film still; rather, it shows him with his friends, also midgets, "at home," in setting and in an intimate grouping of individuals who share the body types and social consequences of being little people. In this family snapshot, made public by Arbus's display of them in an art photograph, Ratoucheff fits perfectly, again suggesting that context is imperative to any subject's status and feelings of belonging or exclusion.

The *Russian Midget* and the *Mexican Dwarf* are performers with stage names, photographed by Arbus in more personal, intimate settings. Both are seated, such that we can't necessarily diagnose their forms of small stature or other possible impairments. Further, Arbus's portraits refuse to typecast them according to conventional personas of little people. Despite the portraits' references to historically constructed, largely fictional characters, these subjects are staged as real people who live in an urban city and work in show business, as did di Morra, Charles Stratton, and Tekki Lomnicki, albeit in different venues. Arbus's portraits frame how these social subjects also embody and confront a dubious and often oppressive legacy of cultural representation.

As in *Jewish Giant*, mythology and fantasy loom large in Arbus's images of little people. In transhistorical myths, literature, fairy tales, and sideshow displays (such as Coney Island), little people known as dwarfs, munchkins, leprechauns, elves, pygmies, Lilliputians, and hobbits and the multiple societies of little creatures created by J. R. R. Tolkien, for examples, are often featured in colonies in which average-sized people are made monstrous, such as Gulliver. These roles typecast little people as childlike, playful, comic, and some, animal-like. These societies are significantly colonized, as in the connections made by freak show anthropological displays between little people and various races of colonized people. Dwarfs, like racial groups, share biological characteristics and certain aspects of physical appearance, qualities often used to stereotype them (most often derogatorily) in character and behavior. Such assignments of social value based on bodies functions to subjugate and marginalize groups according to their differences from dominant groups.

As expressed repeatedly in film and television documentaries and written accounts, social subjects with small stature combat the stereotypes and stock characters constructed of them by culture, which impact their social statuses and the impressions/assumptions made of them by society "at large." Cultural images may also be internalized and cause shame, impacting body images. Often patronizing, such typecasting images effectively disable individuals. The Little People Societies all over the world work to change diminutive and limiting stereotypes of people of small stature and instill pride and group solidarity. The term "little people" affirms their status as real social subjects rather than creatures of fiction. Arbus's photograph points to the power of images of little people in cultural representation and contemporary life, and further points to its own place in that history. Arbus hand printed all of her own images, and her distinctive technique of printing negatives in bold, black frames, a practice begun in 1965, exaggerates the edge, here a visually unstable line, between image and everyday life. Like Witkin's personal touches, this element articulates the false "objectivity" of photography as scientific or documentary evidence, as it calls attention to the manipulations of the photographer through developing and cropping techniques. This portrait articulates its own existence as a venue for display—a staged construction that self-consciously traffics in various representational forms.

Significantly and transgressively, Arbus's image enables Cha Cha to stare back. Although his full, miniature body dominates the frame, Cha Cha's eyes command the greatest attention. *Mexican Dwarf* may present a more clinical format than *Jewish Giant* due to the subject's frontal position, associated, according to artistic convention, with being subjected to a mastering and diagnostic gaze and returning only a compliant look. Yet, Arbus's image exceeds such frames, for Cha Cha not only resigns himself to being viewed, stared at, and perhaps examined, but further, the intensity and ambiguity of his eyes reverse the traditional power dynamics of the gaze. Soliciting the stare in a blend of confrontation, provocation, and flirtation, Cha Cha masters the viewer with his embodied returned gaze. Like the photograph itself, Cha Cha teases the viewer. This multidirectional gaze offers means for interaction between subject, viewer, and photographer, perhaps both disturbingly and optimistically. When one stares at another and is seen in their act of staring, a disruption occurs in spectator/spectacle distance and opposition. Gazes/stares may be faced by uncomfortable glares, or just as likely by smiles. Forcing the viewer to confront their own visual attraction and repulsion, the image asks what motivates gazing/staring and perhaps shakes up a viewer's sense of identification and misrecognition. It engages an intersubjective exchange of multidirectional, and necessarily embodied gazes. Cha Cha performs before the camera in the tradition of a little person as an object on display, but here enacts his own disappearance from an exacting viewer's gaze by offering a facade—a sly withholding, an elusive appearance that maintains anonymity (as aided by the ambiguous props in the margins), holds secrets, and transgresses the frames through shadows.

### Resounding Gazes

Themes of looking and looking back may best characterize Arbus's portraits. Contemporary artist Gillian Wearing writes about Arbus's influence on her work, admiring the images' engagement with the viewer, the inevitable exchange between spectacle and spectator.[34] For Wearing, the subject assumes something from viewers – mesmerizes, possesses, and obsesses them. Judith Butler's (2004) review of the current retrospective of Arbus's work traveling the US and Europe provides further poignant commentary on gazes and facades in the photographs. Butler significantly suggests agency on the part of subjects elsewhere considered disturbing, pathetic, and objectified. She writes about subjects with their eyes closed, such as *Women on the Street with Her Eyes Closed, NYC* (1965) as not "freaks or performers," but rather as revealing something about the "ordinary performance of obduracy."[35] For Butler, a viewer's exacting, possessing, or subjugating gaze is rebuffed and refused; invasion is rejected by a subject's refusal to acknowledge themself as on display. Butler also considers the theme of masks in Arbus's oeuvres, arguing that masked subjects invite, block, and mock the viewer's gaze.

Arbus's *Masked Woman in a Wheelchair* (1970) (a photograph made specifically for colleague and friend Richard Avedon) features a disabled woman, a so-called cripple (perhaps the victim of auto wreck?—some may ask) who attracts attention in the photograph as she would beyond its frames—in the realm of everyday life. She stands out in social life, specifically by not standing. A manual wheelchair, the universal symbol of disability, poses her body, serving as a prop or costume device to tell stories about the woman. The mask she wears becomes another costume piece that accentuates the ultimate failure of the viewer to know, identify, or size up the woman based on her embodiment and based on this image of her; despite the static posing and somewhat institutional building in the blurry background, we are not sure if she is a medical patient, unless we assume this based the wheelchair, nor do we know "what happened," if anything, to her. Arbus's pseudoclinical photograph is insubordinate, like its masked subject, as diagnostic evidence.

This photograph refuses the wheelchair-user to be restrictively typecast. As Arbus's portrait of the anonymous subject and generic title make vivid, the masked woman's specific impairment, identity, history, and social status exceed the frames of the photograph and the wheelchair that frames her body in it. The mask shields her face—the most common bodily feature used to identify and distinguish individuals in physiognomic portraits. The face is considered the visual marker of who one is, and facial features are common targets of exaggeration and manipulation, as Gilman argues (1991) in readings of character from visual images. Here we "see" only her body, although also veiled in consuming clothing and blanket, isolated, centered, set off as characteristic of Arbus's human spectacles. More prominently, we see the wheelchair, which might hint at the characteristic that dominates attention when the woman is stared at by the viewers. Due to the mask she actively holds to her face, we are refused the knowledge of whether she glares, smiles back, mocks us, or closes her eyes in reaction to the stare. She may stubbornly look away, like Carmel, or return an inviting and challenging gaze, like Cha Cha. Here, the woman withholds in an obdurate performance of invisibility, despite that she is on display in the photograph.

Her mask is a multireferential symbol of agency. This mask may articulate Arbus's own social mask; through battles with depression and self-alienation, Arbus may very well have personally identified best with obvious, corporeal social outcasts, rather than with mere "normal" people. The intimate perspective of Arbus's camera with her "freak" subjects may enact her own social mask, which was lifted in liberation from the "normal" standards of life, standards to which Arbus could never conform. The use of a Halloween mask in Arbus's photograph of the wheelchair-user (identified by a small pointed hat at the top with an orange circle, which frames a cartoonish black cat) ushers this mask into contemporary, familiar realms. Halloween is an event with its own alternative subculture and rituals—a time when we escape the confines of our identities and our bodies in acts of play. Arbus's masked woman may be stereotypically "confined" to a wheelchair, according to the conventions of language surrounding wheelchairs and their users; however, the mask mobilizes her agency. The mask enables her becoming and shape-shifting, such that identity is never fixed in the frames or confines of the image, of the wheelchair, or of the body. The mask signifies masquerade; a game of trick or treat; and a means to act, act up, and misbehave, while maintaining a certain level of strategic invisibility. A witch's mask in particular places this woman in a history of legendary deviant and magical female figures, one that also included Arbus. In a display of alchemy, she bewitches, casts spells, and makes objects (in terms of their conventional symbolic meanings) appear and disappear.

In the relationship between cripples and auto wrecks as spectacles, a viewer may desire to look and stare, combined with indig-
nant resistance to identify with the bodies on display. The viewer,
confronted with the "tragedy" of the abnormal other or with the
threat of physical difference and mortality, strives to set limits
and boundaries between bodies. The viewer may aim to maintain
distance and stare at the spectacle to see, in its most exaggerated
form, what the viewer is not, and hopes they will never be. In one
sense then, *Masked Woman in a Wheelchair*, by representing Arbus's
characteristic formal and compositional strategies, turns the tables
on the traditional spectator invisibility versus hypervisibility of the
spectacle on display. The photograph grants the subject on display
the privilege to withhold full visibility, while the subject stares back;
on the other hand, she is on visual display, and in the eyes of many,
exploited in the act of being photographed, as well as in the realms
of everyday life due to her impairment. The photograph allows us a
format in which to stare.

Yet, as I have argued here, Arbus's images are anything but one-
dimensionally objectifying. Butler notes of Arbus's framing of
abnormal bodies that each image presents "a body to be seen and
not had,"[36] such that an externalized, disembodied gaze cannot
possess them. *Masked Woman* then ironically frames the inevitable
reversibility of the gaze through performative, bodily, and artist
acts. The mask may be a metaphor for Arbus's oeuvre of (self-)
portraiture: shape-shifting the body in visual representation, playing with the viewer's expectations of seeing, disrupting multiple
conventions for displaying the body, and endlessly exceeding the
frames. Arbus's images, like the mask, point to the very irony of
the gaze itself—we look at the other in attempts to see ourselves
more clearly, and perhaps may see ourselves best in the eyes of
others. Arbus's work exhibits how the richest moments of discovery result from the appearance of extraordinary disturbances
in the visual field of "normal" and in the exchanges of embodied,
subjective gazes.[37]

# Conclusion

# Staring Back and Forth

Throughout this book, I have argued for the importance of visual culture. Body images and images of the body matter, to individuals, to societies, and to politics. Gazing/staring at bodies articulates, mediates, and informs everyday social interactions, as well as larger social constructions. I have attempted to add dimensions to acts of looking at the body, as a means to encourage viewers to look again. Blending art historical and disability studies perspectives on images of the body, I have showed how disability studies can assert unique viewpoints on art history and how art history can contribute significant contexts to images of disabled bodies. I have foregrounded my own perspective as a viewer and described how viewer perception can affect the power of images. In the process of writing this book, I have also assumed the role of the subject on display.

The subject matter of this book has proved to be personal to me in more ways than one, and in some ways unexpected. I have been physically disabled since birth, involved in studying and making art since childhood, and interested in bridging these subjects in my teaching and writing as an academic professional. And there is more. While researching the beginnings of this book in New York City in the fall of 2004, I visited the Ricco Maresca Gallery for a Joel-Peter Witkin exhibit. I viewed the gallery and met the photography curator, Sarah Hasted, who was as enthusiastic about Witkin's controversial work as I was and was also a personal friend of his. She thought that because of my interest in his work, knowledge of art history, experiences (personal and scholarly) with disability, and, above all, because of my body, Joel and I should meet and collaborate on a photograph. I was eager to serve as his model. After much correspondence and many sketches later, in the spring of 2007, I traveled to Albuquerque, New Mexico, to meet him and to become a performing agent in one of his tableaus.

I wrote about my many experiences in my journal and later, here, in this book. The long weekend is now a blur, but I recall specific details—visiting with Witkin's horses and dogs earlier on the day of the shoot; befriending his wife, Barbara; taking off my prosthesis and my clothes, yet feeling no embarrassment; being painted white to replicate the color of marble sculpture; and posing beside another nude model for different shots. I remember how Witkin would become animated: "That's it!" he'd exclaim, with almost orgasmic excitement. Yet it was all business for him. He was creating his work, which was the source of his fiery pleasure, and we were actors playing roles.

The resulting photograph is titled *Retablo (New Mexico)* (2007) (Figure C.1), referencing Latin American, Catholic folk art traditions (and, for me, many self-portraits by Frida Kahlo). The image was conceived when Witkin saw a retablo image[1] featuring two lesbians embracing, wearing only thongs, and posing above the following retablo prayer:

> San Sebastian, I offer you this retablo because Veronica agreed to come live with me. We are thankful to you for granting us this happiness without having to hide from society to have our relationship. Sylvia M. (translation)

Witkin's photograph also contains this prayer and, of course, fabulist imagery. It is based on this and other similar retablos, printed in France, of homosexuals giving thanks to God and to saints for graces received in their lives. In Witkin's version, Duccio's Christ resists Lucifer's temptations after viewing the future of the world, which includes the tragedy of 9/11. Witkin's composition features a triumphant female nude figure as Vernocia, displaying her corporeal glory and gazing down at her lover, Sylvia, a seated nude figure (me), beside her. We are staged on a pedestal covered in flowing drapery and in front of an elaborate backdrop, which includes a photograph of the same model in a characteristic St Sebastian pose and a painted, shadowed, and winged form confronting a hand

**Figure C.1**    Joel-Peter Witkin, *Retablo (New Mexico)* (2007). Courtesy of the Catherine Edelman Gallery

of salvation. An iconographic reminder of death and a warning symbol of righteousness, a skeleton, lounges comically on the left side of the scene. I cannot logically explain the photograph, as it defies a central narrative. It is far more sensory than sensible. I have my back to the camera and am seated on my two shorted legs (one congenitally amputated above the knee and one below), as I extend my "deformed," or here fabulist/fabulous arms. The female figures are opposing in the positions—one flaunting the front of her nude body, the other much smaller and flaunting her back. The two bodies complement one another and complete a disfigured, heavenly narrative. Witkin said he especially, aesthetically admired my back, which inspired the pose. This seated figure that is me is magical and all-powerful; as viewers stare at my back, I stare back. Like the other models in this book, I perform for my readers/viewers. Life becomes art.

Postscript: Today, a print of the photograph hangs in my living room, I refer to the photographer as Joel, and Paul, my companion on the trip who served as Joel's assistant, is now my husband.

# Notes

## Introduction

1. Hayden Herrera, *Frida Kahlo: The Paintings* (New York: HarperCollins Publishers, 1991).
2. Anne Finger, "Helen and Frida," in *The Disability Studies Reader*, ed. Leonard J. Davis, 401–7 (New York: Routledge, 1997), 403.
3. Major Disability Studies volumes of multidisciplinary critical analysis, personal essays, and poetry include, yet are not limited to the following: Lennard J. Davis, ed., *The Disability Studies Reader* (New York: Routledge, 1997); David T. Mitchell and Sharon L. Snyder, eds., *The Body and Physical Difference: Discourses of Disability* (Ann Arbor: University of Michigan Press, 1997); Mairian Corker and Sally French, eds., *Disability Discourse* (Buckingham UK and Philadelphia, PA: Open University Press, 1999); Susan Crutchfield and Marcy Epstein, eds., *Points of Contact: Disability, Art, and Culture* (Ann Arbor: University of Michigan Press, 2000); Helen Deutsch and Felicity Nussbaum, eds., *"Defects": Engendering the Modern Body* (Ann Arbor: University of Michigan Press, c. 2000); Paul K. Longmore and Lauri Umansky, eds., *The New Disability History: American Perspectives* (New York: New York University Press, 2001); Mairian Corker and Tom Shakespeare, eds., *Disability/Postmodernity: Embodying Disability Theory* (London and New York: Continuum, 2002); and Sharon L. Snyder, Rosemarie Garland-Thomson, and Brenda Jo Brueggemann, *Disability Studies: Enabling the Humanities* (New York: Modern Language Association of America, 2002).
4. For a thorough explanation of medical models and their social and political implications, see Simi Linton, *Claiming Disability: Knowledge and Identity*, foreword by Michael Bérubé (New York and London: New York University Press, 1998).

5. Lennard J. Davis, *Enforcing Normalcy: Disability, Deafness, and the Body* (London and New York: Verso, 1995).
6. See, for examples Alan Gartner and Tom Joe, eds., *Images of the Disabled/Disabling Images* (New York: Praeger, 1987); Martin F. Norden, *The Cinema of Isolation: A History of Physical Disability in the Movies* (New Brunswick, NJ: Rutgers University Press, c. 1994); David T. Mitchell and Sharon L. Snyder, *Narrative Prosthesis: Disability and the Dependencies of Discourse* (Ann Arbor: University of Michigan Press, c. 2000); and Paul K. Longmore, "Screening Stereotypes: Images of Disabled People in Television and Motion Pictures," in *Why I Burned My Book and Other Essays on Disability*, 131–46 (Philadelphia, PA: Temple University Press, 2003).
7. Rosemarie Garland-Thomson, *Extraordinary Bodies: Figuring Physical Disability in American Culture and Literature* (New York: Columbia University Press, 1997).
8. Ibid., *Staring: How We Look* (New York: Oxford University Press, 2009).
9. Lynda Nead, *The Female Nude: Art, Obscenity, and Sexuality* (London and New York: Routledge, 1992).
10. Rosemarie Garland-Thomson, "Seeing the Disabled: Visual Rhetorics of Disability in Popular Photography" in *The New Disability History: American Perspectives*, ed. Paul K. Longmore and Lauri Umansky (New York: New York University Press, 2001), 335–74.
11. Ibid., *Seeing the Disabled*, 339.
12. David Hevey, *The Creatures that Time Forgot* (London and New York: Routledge, 1992).
13. Rosemarie Garland-Thomson, "Staring Back: Self-Representations of Disabled Performance Artists," *American Quarterly* 52, no. 2 (July 2000): 334–38; "Dares to Stares: Disabled Women Performance Artists & the Dynamics of Staring," in *Bodies in Commotion: Disability and Performance*, ed. Carrie Sandahl and Philip Auslander (Ann Arbor: University of Michigan Press, 2005), 30–41.
14. Petra Kuppers. *Disability and Contemporary Performance: Bodies on Edge* (New York and London: Routledge) 2003.
15. Peggy Phelan, *Unmarked: The Politics of Performance* (London: Routledge, 1993). Phelan's argument is rooted in Lacanian

psychoanalysis regarding the primacy of the gaze in formation of identity and social structures of meaning. Underscoring that Lacan proposed the gaze as necessarily social, Phelan explains the codependent dynamics of the gaze, in which one looks at the "other" in order to define the self. The desire to gaze at the "other," Phelan argues, results from the failure to see oneself. For Phelan, Lacan's mirror stage, in which the subject sees itself only as an illusion, serves as a metaphor for how visual images always fail to account for the whole of subjectivity and always reflect more about the desires of the producer and viewer of the images than the body on display.

16. Ibid., 11.

17. Henry M. Sayre, *The Object of Performance: The American Avant-Garde since 1970* (Chicago and London: University of Chicago Press, 1989).

## Chapter 1

1. I viewed this performance in a documentary filmed at the Ann Arbor, Michigan conference, which features interviews and performances by a number of disabled artists, disability studies scholars, and disability rights activists. David Mitchell and Sharon Snyder, directors, *Vital Signs: Crip Culture Talks Back* (A Brace Yourselves Productions, 2000; 1996) (director's cut, 47 minutes).

2. Duffy, in an interview on the videotape, refers specifically to her teachers encouraging her to cover her body: Mitchell and Snyder, *Vital Signs*.

3. Kenneth Clark, *The Nude: A Study in Ideal Form* (New York: Pantheon Books, 1956).

4. Marina Warner, *Monuments and Maidens: The Allegory of the Female Form* (New York: Atheneum, 1985).

5. Peggy Phelan summarizes this narration of the subjugating gaze: "A re-presented woman is always a copy of a copy; the 'real' (of) woman cannot be represented because her function is to re-present man. She is the mirror and thus never in it." Peggy Phelan, *Unmarked: The Politics of Performance* (London: Routledge, 1993), 101.

6. Gaze theory is derived from psychoanalytic theories of Sigmund Freud and Jacques Lacan surrounding the interplays of sight, identity formation, and marginalizing processes of "othering." The gaze has been interrogated predominantly for its dependence on heterosexual desire (in film and extended to other visual media) and construction of sexual difference. See, for examples, Laura Mulvey, "Visual Pleasure and Narrative Cinema" (1975), reprinted in *Visual and Other Pleasures* (Bloomington and Indianapolis: Indiana University Press, 1989); John Berger, *Ways of Seeing* (Middlesex, England: Penguin Books, 1972); and Griselda Pollock, *Vision & Difference: Femininity, Feminism, and the Histories of Art* (London and New York: Routledge, 1988). These discussions have expanded to considerations of how the gaze mediates class (based on the works of Michel Foucault) and brings Foucault's work to analysis of photography, John Tagg. See Foucault, *Discipline and Punish: the Birth of the Prison, Alan Sheridan, trans.* (New York: Vintage Books, 1995, c. 1977) and *The Birth of the Clinic: An Archaeology of Medical Perception*, trans. A. M. Sheridan Smith (New York, Pantheon Books, 1973); And John Tagg, *The Burden of Representation: Essays on Photographies and Histories* (Basingstoke, Hampshire: Macmillan Education, 1988). Many scholars analyze the gaze in relation to racism and constructions of racial difference (See Mary Ann Doane, *Femmes Fatales: Feminism, Film Theory, Psychoanalysis* (New York and London: Routledge, 1991); Linda Nochlin, "The Imaginary Orient," from *The Politics of Vision: Essays on Nineteenth-Century Art and Society* (New York: Harper & Row, c. 1989), 33–59; and Frantz Fanon, *Black Skin, White Masks*, Charles Lam Markmann, trans. (New York : Grove Press, c. 1967).

For a discussion of the gaze in relation to constructions of race and gender in photography see Shawn Michelle Smith, *American Archives: Gender, Race, and Class in Visual Culture* (Princeton, NJ: Princeton University Press, 1999) and *Photography on the Color Line: W.E.B. Du Bois, Race, and Visual Culture* (Durham: Duke University Press, 2004). Such works theorize how the gaze articulates power and produces social hierarchies.

7. Rosemarie Garland-Thomson, "Staring Back: Self-Representations of Disabled Performance Artists," *American Quarterly* 52, no. 2 (July 2000): 334–38.

8. In an article on staring, Garland-Thomson, in reference to visual images brought about by technologies in the nineteenth century, states: "This kind of mediation changes the living staring encounter in several ways; first, it absolves the starer of the responsibility to the object of the stare; second, it eliminates the possibility of engagement between the two people in the staring relationship; third, it grants all agency to the looker and withdraws any agency from the looked upon; fourth, it renders the confrontation static. In short, virtual staring evacuates any dynamism from a lived encounter." See Rosemarie Garland-Thomson, "Staring at the Other," *Disability Studies Quarterly* 25, no. 4 (Fall 2005). (www.dsq-sds.org)

9. Phelan's theories are drawn from the psychoanalysis of Jacques Lacan, whom she argues formulates seeing as social and the gaze as reciprocal and intersubjective.

10. "Amputee" is an ambiguous term that commonly designates anyone born without, having lost, or having so-called deformed limbs.

11. Rosemarie Garland-Thomson, "Seeing the Disabled: Visual Rhetorics of Disability in Popular Photography" in *The New Disability History: American Perspectives*, ed., Paul K. Longmore and Lauri Umansky (New York: New York University Press, 2001), 335–74 and David Hevey, *The Creatures that Time Forgot* (London and New York: Routledge, 1992).

12. Timothy J. Clark, "Preliminaries to a Possible Treatment of 'Olympia,'" from *Art in Modern Culture: An anthology of Critical Texts*, ed. Francis Frascina and Jonathan Harris (New York: HarperCollins Publishers, 1992), 105–20. This essay is a later version of Clark's chapter on Olympia in *The Painting of Modern Life: Paris in the Art of Manet and His Followers* (Princeton, NJ: Princeton University Press, 1984).

13. Rona Goffen, "Sex, Space, and Social History in Titian's Venus of Urbino," in *Titian's "Venus of Urbino,"* ed. Rona Goffen (Cambridge: Cambridge University Press, 1997), 1–22, 63–90.

14. Mary Pardo, "Veiling the Venus of Urbino," in Goffen, 108–28.
15. Clark, "Preliminaries to a Possible Treatment of 'Olympia,'" (1992), 118.
16. Ibid., 116.
17. All the essays in Goffen's collection, including a version of Clark's work on Olympia, agree that what proves fundamentally disturbing in the images (Titian's and Manet's) is the inviting and forcefully returned gaze of the female body. They note also that in the Venus tradition, the female conventionally looked away or lavished her gaze on her male lover, rather than the viewer of the painting.
18. "Hottentot" was a term coined by Dutch settlers to Africa.
19. Baartman was featured as the only human in the text *The History of Mammals* (1826), where she was contextualized with forty-one species of apes. This text was written by one of the founders of teratology, the science of monsters, Geoffrey Saint-Hilaire, and comparative anatomist and prominent French zoologist, Georges Cuvier.
20. Anne Fausto-Sterling, "Gender, Race, and Nation: The Comparative Anatomy of 'Hottentot' Women in Europe, 1815–1817," in *Deviant Bodies Critical Perspectives on Difference in Science and Popular Culture,* ed. Jennifer Terry and Jacqueline Urla (Bloomington: Indiana University Press, 1995), 20.
21. Sander Gilman, "Black Bodies, White Bodies: Toward an Iconography of Female Sexuality in Late Nineteenth-century Art, Medicine, and Literature," in *"Race," Writing, and Difference*, ed. Henry Louis Gates, Jr. (Chicago: University of Chicago Press, 1986), 223–61.
22. Garland-Thomson has discussed the "Hottentot Venus" in relationship to disabled female characters, empowered through their liberation from norms and social standards for beauty, in the resistance literature of contemporary feminist, African-American writers. Rosemarie Garland-Thomson, *Extraordinary Bodies: Figuring Physical Disability in American Culture and Literature* (New York: Columbia University Press, 1997).
23. Cesare Lombroso and Guglielmo Ferrero, *Criminal Woman, the Prostitute, and the Normal Woman*, trans. Nicolce Hahn Rafter and Mary Gibson (Durham, NC: Duke University Press, 2004; 1893).

24. Information on Anne E. Leak-Thompson is drawn mainly from Robert Bogdan, *Freak Show: Presenting Human Oddities for Amusement and Profit* (Chicago: University of Chicago Press, 1988), 217–19.

25. See Rebecca Schneider, *The Explicit Body in Performance* (London and New York: Routledge, 1997) and Amelia Jones, *Body Art/Performing the Subject* (Minneapolis: University of Minnesota, 1998).

26. Schneider, *The Explicit Body in Performance*.

27. Kenneth Clark, *The Nude: A Study in Ideal Form* (New York: Pantheon Books, 1956).

28. Warner, *Monuments and Maidens*.

29. Duffy's photographic series *Cutting the Ties that Bind* (1987) was also featured in the exhibition "Vis-Ability: Views from the Interior" at the Slusser Gallery at the University of Michigan (May and June of 1995). The series is discussed by Lennard J. Davis, and one of the photographs graces the cover of his book: Lennard J. Davis, "Visualizing the Disabled Body: The Classical Nude and the Fragmented Torso," in *Enforcing Normalcy*, 126–57. Duffy has written two short pieces on these photographs as well: Mary Duffy, "Redressing the Balance," *Feminist Art News* 3, no. 8 (1991): 15–18 and "Cutting the Ties that Bind," *Feminist Art News* 2, no. 10 (1989): 6–7.

30. Printed in Lennard B. Davis, ed., *Disability Studies Reader* (New York: Routledge, 1997), 408–9.

31. Wade's performances are sampled on the video that features Duffy's performance: Mitchell and Snyder, directors (2000; 1996).

32. Mitchell and Snyder, *My Hands* (2001[1996]).

33. Marina Warner, *From the Beast to the Blonde* (New York: Farrar, Straus, and Giroux, 1995).

34. Garland-Thomson, *Staring Back*, 334–38.

35. Audre Lorde, "The Transformation of Silence into Language and Action," in *Sister Outsider* (Santa Cruz, CA: Crossing Press, 1984), 40–44.

36. Mitchell and Snyder, (2000; 1996) and Bonnie Sherr Klein, *Shameless: The Art of Disability* (National Film Board of Canada, 2006).

## Chapter 2

1. Examples of other public art projects in Britain that resulted from 1980s and 1990s initiatives are: Victoria Square, Birmingham; Broadgate Business Park; Cardiff Bay, Birmingham; London Docklands, and various projects gracing transportation stations, hospitals, and parks. See Sara Selwood, *The Benefits of Public Art: The Polemics of Public Places* (Poole, UK: Policy Studies Institute Publications, 1995).

2. The Fourth Plinth Project is under the auspices of the Mayor of London and sponsored by the Arts Council of England. Information is available at: http://www.fourthplinth.co.uk/

3. Malcolm Miles, *Art, Space, and the City: Public Art and Urban Futures* (London and New York: Rutledge, 1997), 58.

4. Suzanne Lacy, ed., *Mapping the Terrain: New Genre Public Art* (Seattle, WA: Bay Press, 1995).

5. Lapper is quoted on the Fourth Plinth Project website http://www.fourthplinth.co.uk/.

6. Lapper, quoted in Staff and agencies, "Livingstone unveils statue of 'modern heroine,'" *Guardian* (Thursday September 15, 2005).

7. Maev Kennedy, "Pregnant and proud: Statue of artist wins place in Trafalgar Square," *Guardian* (Tuesday March 16, 2004).

8. For example, see Adrian Searle, "Arresting, strange and beautiful," *Guardian* (Friday September 16, 2005).

9. Marina Warner, *Monuments and Maidens: The Allegory of the Female Form* (New York: Atheneum, 1985).

10. Interestingly, Lapper has expressed her reservations about the sculptural form of Quinn's statue. In her memoir, she describes an exhibit of Quinn's work that included macquettes for *Alison Lapper Pregnant*, which she attended at Cube2 Gallery: "After looking at the statues for a while I realized something. The marble had no life in it, no personality. I was very excited and happy to be there but I felt divorced from the statues themselves. The statues seemed to me more like death masks. It's what I imagined I would look like if I was dead. So it was like walking around a dead, quiet Alison Lapper. Not like me at all. The one thing I loved about the statues, though, was that they sparkled. The gleaming white marble had that quality to it and

in that respect, because I love sparkly things, it reflected me very well." Alison Lapper (with Guy Feldman), *My Life in My Hands* (London and New York: Simon & Schuster UK, 2005), 243.

11. Waldemar Januszczak, "Matter of life and death—Art—Profile—Marc Quinn," *Sunday Times*, December 10, 2000.
12. Robert Preece, "Just a Load of Shock? An Interview with Marc Quinn," *Sculpture* 19, no. 8 (October 2000): 14–19.
13. William Cederwell, "What they said about . . . the fourth plinth," *Guardian* (Thursday March 18, 2004).
14. Preece, "Just a Load of Shock? An Interview with Marc Quinn."
15. Jonathan Jones, "Bold, graphic, subversive—but bad art," *Guardian* (Tuesday March 16, 2004).
16. Livingstone, quoted in "Livingstone unveils statue of 'modern heroine."
17. Kim Q. Hall, "Pregnancy, Disability and Gendered Embodiment: Rethinking Alison Lapper Pregnant," lecture delivered at the Society for Disability Studies Conference, Bethesda, MD, June 17, 2006.
18. London Mayor Ken Livingstone is quoted on the Fourth Plinth Project website http://www.fourthplinth.co.uk/.
19. Preece, "Just a Load of Shock? An Interview with Marc Quinn."
20. Mark Gisbourne, "The Self and Others" *Contemporary (U.K.)* no. 2 (February 2002): 52–57.
21. Martin Kemp, Marina Wallace, Hayward Gallery, and Anderson-Riggins Memorial Fund. *Spectacular Bodies: The Art and Science of the Human Body from Leonardo to Now* (London, Hayward Gallery; Los Angeles: University of California Press, 2000).
22. Lapper, *My Life in My Hands*, 237.
23. Preece, "Just a Load of Shock? An Interview with Marc Quinn."
24. Waldemar Januszczak, "Matter of life and death—Art—Profile—Marc Quinn," *Sunday Times* (December 10, 2000).
25. Hanne Olsen, letter to the editor, "More than a message," *Guardian* (Saturday March 20, 2004).
26. Charles L. Griswold, "The Vietnam Veterans Memorial and the Washington Mall: Philosophical Thoughts on Political Iconography," in *Critical Issues in Public Art: Content, Context,*

*and Controversy*, ed. Harriet F. Seine and Sally Webster (Washington and London: Smithsonian Institute Press, 1992), 71–100.

27. Alice Thomson of the *Daily Telegraph* was quoted in Cederwell.
28. Lapper, *My Life in My Hands*, 236.
29. Ibid., 234.
30. Miles, *Art, Space, and the City*.
31. Rodney Mace, *Trafalgar Square: Emblem of Empire* (Southampton, UK: Camelot Press, 1976).
32. This opinion was expressed, for example, in the following newspaper quote: "Roy Hattersley, in the Daily Mail, agreed that while the sculpture was 'a celebration of both courage and motherhood', it was nevertheless 'the wrong statue in the wrong place.' The Trafalgar Square plinth is crying out for 'individual examples of national achievement and British greatness,' he said. Hattersley drew up his own shortlist of likely greats, including Shakespeare, Milton, Elgar, Newton and Wren. 'Most of us will share the view that Lapper is someone to admire . . . but the simple truth is that Trafalgar Square is meant for something else.' Cederwell.
33. Jeanette Hart, letter to the editor, *Guardian* (Wednesday September 21, 2005).
34. Paul Usherwood, "The Battle of Trafalgar Square," *Art Monthly* 2 no. 4 (March 2004), 43.
35. Mace, *Trafalgar Square*.
36. These are qualities of successful, transformative public art advocated by art critic Patricia Phillips. Patricia C. Phillips, "Temporality and Public Art," in *Critical Issues in Public Art: Content, Context, and Controversy*, ed. Harriet F. Senie and Sally Webster (Washington and London: Smithsonian Institute Press, 1992), p. 295–304.
37. Ibid., 296–97.
38. Andrew Crooks, letter to the editor, *Guardian* (Wednesday March 17, 2004).
39. Lapper, *My Life in My Hands*, 169–70.
40. Ibid., 237.
41. Adrian Searle, *The Guardian*, Friday September 16, 2005.

42. Portions of this chapter have been reprinted, with permission, from the following:
    Ann Millett, "Sculpting Body Ideals: *Alison Lapper Pregnant* and the Public Display of Disability," in *Disability Studies Quarterly* 28, no. 3 (Summer 2008), and in *The Disability Studies Reader*, 3rd ed., (New York: Routledge, 2010).

## Chapter 3

1. Rosemarie Garland-Thomson, "Seeing the Disabled: Visual Rhetorics of Disability in Popular Photography," in *The New Disability History: American Perspectives*, ed. Paul K. Longmore and Laurie Umansky, (New York: New York University Press, 2000), 335–74.
2. Eugenia Parry, *Joel-Peter Witkin* (London and New York: Phaidon, 2001), 115.
3. Quoted from a discussion in September 2004 with Sarah Hasted, Director of Photography at the Ricco-Maresca Gallery, and now Director of the Hasted-Hunt Gallery, New York.
4. My summaries of other critics' analyses of Witkin's work are drawn from the following sources: Max Kozloff, "Contention between Two Critics about a Disagreeable Beauty," *Artforum* 22 (February 1984): 45–53; Cynthia Chris, "Witkin's Others," *Exposure* 26, no. 1 (Spring 1988): 16–26, 23–24; Marlene Schnelle-Schneyder, "Joel-Peter Witkin: Dream Work in Staged Pictures—The Demythologized World of Joel-Peter Witkin," *Camera Austria* 35 (1990): 30–36; Brooks Adams, "Grotesque Photography," *Print Collector's Newsletter* 21, no. 6 (January–February 1991): 206–10; Max Kozloff, "Stilled Lives," *Artforum* 31 (Summer 1993): 75–79; R. H. Cravens, "Joel-Peter Witkin," *Aperture* no. 133 (Fall 1993); Germano Celant, *Joel-Peter Witkin* (Milan: Edizioni Charta, 1995); Maria Christina Villaseñor, "The Witkin Carnival," *Performing Arts Journal* 18, no. 2 (May 1996): 77–82; Eleanor Heartney, "Postmodern Heretics," *Art in America* 85, no. 2 (Feb. 1997): 32–35, 37; Ivan Berry (interviewer), "The Marriage of Heaven and Hell: Joel-Peter Witkin," *Art Papers* 22, no. 6 (November–December 1998): 34–39;

Rachelle Dermer, "Joel-Peter Witkin and Dr. Stanley B. Burns: A Language of Body Parts," *History of Photography* 23, no. 3 (Autumn 1999): 245–53, 248; Peter Schwenger, "Corpsing the Image," *Critical Inquiry* 26, no. 3 (Spring 2000): 395–413; and Brett Wood, "Photo Mortis: Resurrecting Photographs of Crime and Death," *Art Papers* 24, no. 2 (March–April 2000): 18–23.

5. See, for example, Roland Barthes, *Camera Lucida: Reflections on Photography*, trans. Richard Howard (New York: Hill and Wang, 1981); John Tagg, *The Burden of Representation: Essays on Photographies and Histories* (Basingstoke, Hampshire: Macmillan Education, 1988); and Abigail Solomon-Godeau, *Photography at the Dock: Essays on Photographic History, Institutions, and Practices* (Minneapolis: University of Minnesota Press, c. 1991).

6. Witkin edited a volume of Burns' collection: *Masterpieces of Medical Photography: Selections from the Burns Archive*, ed. Joel-Peter Witkin, captions by Stanley B. Burns (Pasadena, CA: Twelvetrees Press, 1987) and curated the exhibit, from which the following catalogue was published:, Joel-Peter Witkin, ed., *Harms Way: Lust & Madness, Murder & Mayhem: A Book of Photographs* (Santa Fe, NM: Twin Palms Publishers, 1994). I put the last name last to be consistent with all the other endnotes, but I realize the bibliography is in reverse. Should all the endnotes be edited?

7. Ambroise Paré, *On Monsters and Marvels*, trans. Janis L. Pallister (Chicago: University of Chicago Press, 1982; 1840).

8. See Leslie Fiedler, *Freaks: Myths and Images of the Secret Self* (New York: Simon & Schuster, 1978). Like Paré, Fiedler organizes his book according to freakish "types" or corporealities.

9. George M. Gould and Walter L. Pyle, *Anomalies and curiosities of medicine: being an encyclopedic collection of rare and extraordinary cases, and of the most striking instances of abnormality in all branches of medicine and surgery, derived from an exhaustive research of medical literature from its origin to the present day, abstracted, classified, annotated, and indexed* (New York, Julian Press 1956; 1896).

10. One particularly illuminating example in Gould and Pyle is the section titled "Physiological and Functional Anomalies,"

which includes (among random others) anomalies of body fluids, fetishism, juggling, fire worship, ventriloquism, strong men (modern Hercules), chronic opium eating, divers, runners, spontaneous combustion of the body, contortionism, acrobats, tightrope walkers, morbid desire for pain, bulimia, death from joy and laughter (used as arguments for rational, unemotional behavior), cannibals, artificial manufacture of "wild boys," magnetic, phosphorescent, and electric anomalies, deafness (Helen Keller included), blindness, and the "extraordinary compensation" of other senses in affect.

11. For many examples of the themes and functions of anatomical and surgical displays in art history, see Martin Kemp, Marina Wallace, Hayward Gallery, and Anderson-Riggins Memorial Fund, *Spectacular Bodies: The Art and Science of the Human Body from Leonardo to Now* (London, Hayward Gallery; Los Angeles: University of California Press, 2000). In her discussion of dissection and art, Barbara Maria Stafford writes that the Renaissance flowering of artistic and scientific studies of anatomy and Classical philosophies reached a zenith in the Enlightenment and emerged in art theory and practices, including physiognomic studies, portraiture, and still life. In addition, dissection practices and metaphors, according to Stafford, informed visual displays of bodies in medical and freak venues and other forms of vernacular culture. Anatomy lessons, dissection, and sketching from live and wax models and from medical illustrations were prominent in academic painting instruction since the Renaissance. Barbara Maria Stafford, *Body Criticism: Imaging the Unseen in Enlightenment Art and Medicine* (Cambridge, MA: MIT Press, 1991), 47–129. In addition, Lynda Nead has argued that such histories of art training initially focused on medical displays of male bodies and shifted to females in the nineteenth century. Lynda Nead, *The Female Nude: Art, Obscenity, and Sexuality* (London and New York: Routledge, 1992).

12. Stafford, *Body Criticism*, 107–8.

13. Lennard J. Davis, *Enforcing Normalcy: Disability, Deafness, and the Body* (London and New York: Verso, 1995).

14. Allan Sekula, "The Body and the Archive," *October* 39 (Winter 1998): 3–64.

15. Daniel M. Fox and Christopher Lawrence, *Photographing Medicine: Images and Power in Britain and America Since 1840* (New York; Westport, CT; London: Greenwood Press, 1988), 54. See also Stanley B. Burns, *Early Medical Photography in America (1939–1883)* (New York: Burns Archive, 1983).

16. Burns (1983) writes that the higher the social status of the patient, the more likely they were draped, and patients who were photographed over time to document their treatments were generally clothed in continuously improving styles to indicate their "progress" of rehabilitation or cure. In relation, military officers were most often photographed in their uniforms to indicate rank, whereas enlisted men wore close to nothing in their medical photographs, 1262.

17. Such differentiations between the erotic versus the pornographic are made, for example, by Barthes.

18. Gilman argues that photography constructs and informs histories of mental illness, disability, asylums, institutionalization, and evolution. See Sander L. Gilman, *Picturing Health and Illness: Images of Identity and Difference* (Baltimore: Johns Hopkins University Press, c. 1995).

19. Shawn Michelle Smith, *American Archives: Gender, Race, and Class in Visual Culture* (Princeton, NJ: Princeton University Press, 1999).

20. Tagg, *The Burden of Representation*.

21. David Lomas, "Body languages: Kahlo and medical imagery," in *The Body Imaged: The Human Form and Visual Culture since the Renaissance*, ed. Kathleen Adler and Marcia R. Pointon (Cambridge and New York: Cambridge University Press, 1993), 5–19.

22. Georges Bataille, "The Big Toe," in *Visions of Excess: Selected Writings, 1927–1939*, ed. and trans. Allan Stoekl (Minneapolis: University of Minnesota Press, 1985), 20–23.

23. Stanley B. Burns, *A Morning's Work: Medical Photographs from the Burns Archive & Collection 1843–1939* (Santa Fe, NM: Twin Palms Publishers, 1998).

24. For examples: Kozloff, "Stilled Lives" and "Contention between Two Critics about a Disagreeable Beauty;" Chris, "Witkin's Others;" and Villaseñor, "The Witkin Carnival."

25. Peggy Phelan, *Unmarked: The Politics of Performance* (London: Routledge, 1993).
26. Robert Bogdan, *Freak Show: Presenting Human Oddities for Amusement and Profit* (Chicago: University of Chicago Press, 1988), 220.
27. See Marie-Hélène Huet, *Monstrous Imagination* (Cambridge, MA: Harvard University Press, 1993) and Paré, *On Monsters and Marvels*.
28. Lorraine Daston and Katharine Park, *Wonders and the Order of Nature, 1150–1750* (New York: Zone Books; Cambridge, MA: Distributed by the MIT Press, 1998). Also see Fiedler, *Freaks*; Bogdan, *Freak Show*; Rosemarie Garland-Thomson, ed., *Freakery: Cultural Spectacles of the Extraordinary Body* New York: New York University Press, 1996); and Rachel Adams, *Sideshow USA: Freaks and the American Cultural Imagination* (Chicago: University of Chicago Press, 2001).
29. John D. Stoeckle and George Abbott White, *Plain Pictures of Plain Doctoring: Vernacular Expression in New Deal Medicine and Photography: 80 Photographs from the Farm Security Administration* (Cambridge, MA: MIT Press, c. 1985), 111.
30. Portions of this chapter have been reprinted, with permission, from Ann Millett, "Performing Amputation: The Photographs of Joel-Peter Witkin," in *Text and Performance Quarterly*, 28, no. 1, 8 (January 2008), 8–42. (http://www.informaworld.com)

## Chapter 4

1. Judith Goldman, "Diane Arbus: The Gap Between Intention and Effect," *Art Journal* 34, no. 1 (Fall 1974): 30–35; Susan Sontag, *On Photography* (New York: Farrar, Straus, and Giroux, 1977); and David Hevey, *The Creatures that Time Forgot* (London and New York: Routledge, 1992).
2. Arbus worked for various magazines and newspapers, such as *Harper's Bazarre, The Sunday Times, Esquire, Nova, Essence, Glamour, Seventeen, Vogue, Life, Newsweek*, some in collaborations with her husband, Allen, and others independently. See Patricia Bosworth, *Diane Arbus: A Biography* (New York: Alfred A. Knopf, 1984).

3. Doon Arbus, "Afterword," in *Untitled/Diane Arbus,* ed. Doon Arbus and Yolanda Cuomo (New York: Aperture, c. 1995) and Judith Butler, "Surface Tensions," *Artforum* 42, no. 5 (February 2004): 199–224.

4. Goldman, "Diane Arbus"; Sontag, *On Photography*; and Bosworth, *Diane Arbus.*

5. Goldman, "Diane Arbus," 30.

6. Arbus (1972) and in "Revisiting the Icons: The Intimate Photography of Diane Arbus," *Harper's Magazine* 307, no. 1842 (November 2003): 84–88.

7. Butler, "Surface Tensions."

8. Hevey, *The Creatures that Time Forgot.*

9. Goldman, "Diane Arbus," 30.

10. Acromegaly differs from "Giantism" as a condition of overactive production of the pituitary glad. Most subjects with acromegaly are born average size and experience rapid growth spurts at early age, have chronic swelling, like Carmel, and often have leg problems. Another distinguishing characteristic of acromegaly is enlarged facial features.

11. Jenny Carchman (reporter and narrator), *The Jewish Giant: A Sound Portrait* (New York: Sound Portraits Productions, 1999). (Premiered on NPR's *All Things Considered* October 6, 1999).

12. Daniel P. Mannix, *Freaks: We Who Are Not as Others* (New York: RE/Search Publications, 1999; 1969).

13. Carchman, *The Jewish Giant.*

14. Rachel Adams, *Sideshow USA: Freaks and the American Cultural Imagination* (Chicago: University of Chicago Press, 2001).

15. According to Michael Mitchell, the nineteenth-century technical advancements in photography, such as image quality and reproduction capabilities, that resulted in the carte de visite and cabinet portrait forms also enabled full-body portraits, because of the increased clarity of detail. Previously, portraits had conventionally been ¾ bust images. See Michael Mitchell, *Monsters: Human Freaks in America's Gilded Age, the Photographs of Chas. Eisenmann* (Toronto, Canada: ECW Press, 2002), 22.

16. Rosamond Purcell, *Special Cases: Natural Anomalies and Historical Monsters* (San Francisco: Chronicle Books, c. 1997). The photograph is featured on page 103. The Museum displays a medical collection that Thomas Dent Mütter purchased in

1874 from Dr. Josef Hyrtl, a professor of anatomy and collector of medical and anthropological specimens of "anomalies" or "pathological" cases in Vienna in the mid-nineteenth century. The collection features many skeletons and skulls in a variety of cranial shapes.

17. This image is printed in Leslie Fiedler, *Freaks: Myths and Images of the Secret Self* (New York: Simon & Schuster, 1978), 104.

18. Mitchell writes that as the conventions of cartes de visites progressed, the settings got more minimal to offset the magnificence of the body.

19. This remark is drawn from a postcard to Peter Crookston, dated May 1968, and printed in Diane Arbus and San Francisco Museum of Modern Art, *Diane Arbus: Revelations*, 1st ed. (New York: Random House, 2003), 190.

20. M. M. Bakhtin, *Rabelais and His World* (Cambridge: MIT Press, 1968).

21. Fiedler, *Freaks*, 91.

22. Sander Gilman, *The Jew's Body* (New York: Routledge, 1991).

23. Gould and Pyle, *Anomalies and curiosities of medicine*, 324–25.

24. François Rabelais, *The Portable Rabelais*, edited and translated by Samuel Putnam (New York: Penguin Books, 1979; 1929), 53.

25. See Stanley B. Burns, *A Morning's Work: Medical Photographs from the Burns Archive & Collection, 1843–1939*, 1st ed. (Santa Fe, NM: Twin Palms, 1998).

26. Robert Bogdan, *Freak Show: Presenting Human Oddities for Amusement and Profit* (Chicago: University of Chicago Press, 1988).

27. Mannix, *Freaks*, 22.

28. Lynda Nead characterizes pornography as making private acts public. Lynda Nead, *The Female Nude: Art, Obscenity, and Sexuality* (London and New York: Routledge, 1992), 100–101.

29. Arbus attended the annual picnic for the Federation of the Handicapped on July 10, 1971, by request of a written invitation that she received from the group.

30. American studies scholar and cultural theorist Shawn Michelle Smith draws this assessment from Walter Benjamin's discussion of Sanders' work in his 1930 essay "A Small History of Photography." See Shawn Michelle Smith, *American Archives:*

*Gender, Race, and Class in Visual Culture* (Princeton, NJ: Princeton University Press, 1999).

31. Printed in *Revelations*, 177.
32. Arbus articulated her thoughts upon the closing of the museum: "It used to be that if, as your mother would say, you didn't know what to do with yourself, you would do it at the Hubert's Museum. You'd . . . descend, somewhat like Orpheus or Alice or Virgil, into the cellar which was where Hubert's Museum was . . . Coming into the unholy fluorescent glare of it you'd see yourself dwarfed and fattened and stretched into several distorting mirrors and all around you like flowers a thousand souvenirs of human aberrations, as if the world had quite literally stashed away down there everything it didn't need." Quoted in *Revelations*, 177.
33. Bosworth, *Diane Arbus*.
34. Gillian Wearing, "The Eyes Have It," *Artforum* 42, no. 5 (February 2004): 125.
35. Butler, "Surface Tensions," 120.
36. Ibid.
37. Portions of this chapter have been reprinted, with permission, from the following: Ann Millett, "Exceeding the Frame: The Photography of Diane Arbus," in *Disability Studies Quarterly* 24, no. 4 (Fall 2004).

## Conclusion

1. "Infinitas Gracias," editions du Seuil, France, 2004, 162.

# Selected Bibliography

Adams, Brooks. "Grotesque Photography." *Collector's Newsletter* 21, no. 6 (January–February 1991): 206–10.

Adams, Rachel. *Sideshow USA: Freaks and the American Cultural Imagination.* Chicago: University of Chicago Press, 2001.

Adler, K., and M. R. Pointon, ed. *The Body Imaged: The Human Form and Visual Culture since the Renaissance.* Cambridge; New York: Cambridge University Press, 1993.

Arbus, Diane, and the San Francisco Museum of Modern Art. *Diane Arbus: Revelations,* 1st ed. New York: Random House, 2003.

Arbus, Doon, and Yolanda Cuomo. *Untitled/Diane Arbus.* New York: Aperture, c. 1995.

Bakhtin, M. M. *Rabelais and His World.* Cambridge, MA: MIT Press, 1968.

Barthes, Roland. *Camera Lucida: Reflections on Photography.* Translated by Richard Howard. New York: Hill and Wang, 1981.

Bataille, Georges. *Visions of Excess: Selected Writings, 1927–1939.* Edited and translated by Allan Stoekl. Minneapolis: University of Minnesota Press, 1985.

Berger, John. *Ways of Seeing.* Middlesex, England: Penguin Books, 1972.

Berry, Ivan (interviewer). "The Marriage of Heaven and Hell: Joel-Peter Witkin," *Art Papers* 22, no. 6 (November–December 1998): 34–39.

Blocker, Jane. *What the Body Cost: Desire, History and Performance.* Minneapolis and London: University of Minnesota Press, 2004.

Bogdan, Robert. *Freak Show: Presenting Human Oddities for Amusement and Profit.* Chicago: University of Chicago Press, 1988.

Bordo, Susan. *The Flight to Objectivity: Essays on Cartesianism & Culture*. Albany: State University of New York Press, 1987.

Bosworth, Patricia. *Diane Arbus: A Biography*. New York: Alfred A. Knopf, 1984.

Bryson, Norman. "House of Wax." In *Cindy Sherman, 1975–1993*. Krauss, Rosalind with an essay by Norman Bryson, 216–23. New York: Rizzoli, 1993.

———. *Looking at the Overlooked: Four Essays on Still Life Painting*. Cambridge, MA: Harvard University Press, 1990.

Burns, Stanley B., *Early Medical Photography in America (1939–1883)*. New York: Burns Archive, 1983.

———. *A Morning's Work: Medical Photographs from the Burns Archive & Collection 1843–1939*. Santa Fe, NM: Twin Palms Publishers, 1998.

Butler, Judith. "Surface Tensions," *Artforum* 42, no. 5 (February 2004): 199–224.

Carchman, Jenny (reporter and narrator). *The Jewish Giant: A Sound Portrait*. New York: Sound Portraits Productions, 1999.

Cederwell, William. "What they said about . . . the fourth plinth," *Guardian* (Thursday March 18, 2004).

Celant, Germano. *Joel-Peter Witkin*. Milan: Edizioni Charta, 1995.

Chris, Cynthia. "Witkin's Others," *Exposure* 26, no. 1 (Spring 1988): 16–26, 23–24.

Clark, Kenneth. *The Nude: A Study in Ideal Form*. New York: Pantheon Books, 1956.

Clark, Timothy J. *The Painting of Modern Life: Paris in the Art of Manet and His Followers*. Princeton, NJ: Princeton University Press, 1984.

———. "Preliminaries to a Possible Treatment of 'Olympia.'" In *Art in Modern Culture: An Anthology of Critical Texts*, edited by F. Frascina and J. Harris, 105–20. New York: HarperCollins Publishers, 1992.

Corker, Mairian, and Sally French, eds. *Disability Discourse*. Buckingham, UK and Philadelphia, PA: Open University Press, 1999.

Corker, Mairian, and Tom Shakespeare, eds. *Disability/Postmodernity: Embodying Disability Theory*. London and New York: Continuum, 2002.

Cravens, R. H. "Joel-Peter Witkin," *Aperture* no. 133 (Fall 1993).

Crutchfield, Susan, and Marcy Epstein, eds. *Points of Contact: Disability, Art, and Culture.* Ann Arbor: The University of Michigan Press, 2000.

Daston, L, and K. Park. *Wonders and the Order of Nature, 1150–1750.* New York: Zone Books; Cambridge, MA: Distributed by the MIT Press, 1998.

Davis, Lennard J., ed. *The Disability Studies Reader.* New York: Routledge, 1997.

———. *Enforcing Normalcy: Disability, Deafness, and the Body.* London and New York: Verso, 1995.

Debord, Guy. *The Society of the Spectacle.* New York: Zone Books, 1994.

Dentith, Simon. *Bakhtinian Thought: An Introductory Reader.* London and New York: Routledge, 1995.

Dermer, Rachelle. "Joel-Peter Witkin and Dr. Stanley B. Burns: A Language of Body Parts." *History of Photography* 23, no. 3 (Autumn 1999): 245–53, 248.

Derrida, Jacques. *The Truth in Painting.* Translated by G. Bennington and I. McLeod. Chicago: University of Chicago Press, 1987.

Deutsch, Helen, and Felicity Nussbaum, eds. *"Defects": Engendering the Modern Body.* Ann Arbor: University of Michigan Press, c. 2000.

Doane, Mary Ann. *Femmes Fatales: Feminism, Film Theory, Psychoanalysis.* New York and London: Routledge, 1991.

DuBois, Page. *Sappho is Burning.* Chicago: University of Chicago Press, 1995.

Duffy, Mary. "Cutting the Ties that Bind," *Feminist Art News* 2, no. 10 (1989): 6–7.

———. "Redressing the Balance," *Feminist Art News* 3, no. 8 (1991): 15–18.

Fanon, Frantz. *Black Skin, White Masks.* Translated by Charles Lam Markmann. New York: Grove Press, c. 1967.

Fiedler, Leslie. *Freaks: Myths and Images of the Secret Self.* New York: Simon & Schuster, 1978.

Fox, D. M., and C. Lawrence. *Photographing Medicine: Images and Power in Britain and America since 1840.* New York; Westport, CT; London: Greenwood Press, 1988.

Garland-Thomson, Rosemarie. "Dares to Stares: Disabled Women Performance Artists & the Dynamics of Staring." In *Bodies in*

*Commotion: Disability and Performance,* edited by C. Sandahl and P. Auslander, 30–41. Ann Arbor: University of Michigan Press, 2005.

———. *Extraordinary Bodies: Figuring Physical Disability in American Culture and Literature.* New York: Columbia University Press, 1997.

———. ed. *Freakery: Cultural Spectacles of the Extraordinary Body.* New York: New York University Press, 1996.

———. "Seeing the Disabled: Visual Rhetorics of Disability in Popular Photography." In *The New Disability History: American Perspectives,* edited by P. K. Longmore and L. Umansky, 335–74. New York: New York University Press, 2001.

———. *Staring: How We Look.* New York: Oxford University Press, 2009.

———. "Staring Back: Self-Representations of Disabled Performance Artists." *American Quarterly* 52, no. 2 (July 2000): 334–38.

Gartner, Alan, and Tom Joe, eds. *Images of the Disabled/Disabling Images.* New York: Praeger, 1987.

Gilman, Sander. "Black Bodies, White Bodies: Toward an Iconography of Female Sexuality in Late Nineteenth-century Art, Medicine, and Literature." In *"Race," Writing, and Difference,* edited by Henry Louis Gates, Jr., 223–61. Chicago: University of Chicago Press, 1986.

———. *The Jew's Body.* New York: Routledge, 1991.

———. *Picturing Health and Illness: Images of Identity and Difference.* Baltimore: Johns Hopkins University Press, c. 1995.

Gisbourne, Mark. "The Self and Others." *Contemporary (U.K.)* no. 2 (February 2002): 52–57.

Goffen, Rona, ed. *Titian's "Venus of Urbino."* Cambridge: Cambridge University Press, 1997.

Goffman, Erving. *The Presentation of Self in Everyday Life.* New York: Doubleday Anchor Books, 1959.

———. *Stigma: Notes on the Management of a Spoiled Identity.* New York: Simon and Schuster, 1963.

Goldman, Judith. "Diane Arbus: The Gap between Intention and Effect." *Art Journal* 34, no. 1 (Fall 1974): 30–35.

Gould, G. M., and W. L. Pyle. *Anomalies and curiosities of medicine: being an encyclopedic collection of rare and extraordinary cases, and of the most striking instances of abnormality in all branches of medicine and surgery, derived from an exhaustive research of medical literature from its origin to the present day, abstracted, classified, annotated, and indexed.* New York, Julian Press 1956; 1896.

Grosz, Elizabeth. *Volatile Bodies: Toward a Corporeal Feminism.* Bloomington and Indianapolis: Indiana University Press, 1994.

Hall, Kim Q. "Pregnancy, Disability and Gendered Embodiment: Rethinking Alison Lapper Pregnant," lecture delivered at the Society for Disability Studies Conference, Bethesda, MD, June 17, 2006.

Heartney, Eleanor. "Postmodern Heretics," *Art in America* 85, no. 2 (February 1997): 32–35, 37.

Herrera, Hayden. *Frida: A Biography of Frida Kahlo.* New York Harper & Row Publishers, 1983.

———. *Frida Kahlo: The Paintings.* New York: HarperCollins Publishers, 1991.

Hevey, David. *The Creatures that Time Forgot.* London and New York: Routledge, 1992.

Huet, Marie-Hélène. *Monstrous Imagination.* Cambridge, MA: Harvard University Press, 1993).

Hutchinson, Ray, ed. *Constructions of Urban Space.* Stamford, CT: Jai Press, 2000.

Januszczak, Waldemar. "Matter of life and death—Art—Profile— Marc Quinn," *Sunday Times* (December 10, 2000).

Jay, Ricky. *Learned Pigs & Fireproof Women.* New York: Villard Books, 1986.

Jones, Amelia. *Body Art/Performing the Subject.* Minneapolis: University of Minnesota, 1998.

Jones, Jonathan. "Bold, graphic, subversive—but bad art," *Guardian* (Tuesday March 16, 2004).

Kemp, Martin, and Marina Wallace. *Spectacular Bodies: The Art and Science of the Human Body from Leonardo to Now.* London, Hayward Gallery; Los Angeles: University of California Press, 2000.

Kennedy, Maev. "Pregnant and proud: Statue of artist wins place in Trafalgar Square," *Guardian* (Tuesday March 16, 2004).

Klein, Bonnie Sherr. *Shameless: The Art of Disability.* National Film Board of Canada, 2006.

Kozloff, Max. "Contention between Two Critics about a Disagreeable Beauty," *Artforum* 22 (February 1984): 45–53.

————. "Stilled Lives," *Artforum* 31 (Summer 1993): 75–79.

Kuppers, Petra. *Disability and Contemporary Performance: Bodies on Edge*. New York and London: Routledge, 2003.

Lacan, Jacques. "The mirror stage as formative of the function of the I," in *Ecrits: a Selection, 1966*, translated by Alan Sheridan, 1–7. New York: W. W. Norton & Company, 1977.

Lacy, Suzanne, ed. *Mapping the Terrain: New Genre Public Art*. Seattle, WA: Bay Press, 1995.

Lapper, Alison. *My Life in My Hands*. London and New York: Simon & Schuster UK, 2005.

Lewis, Michael. *Shame: The Exposed Self*. New York: The Free Press, A Division of Macmillan, 1992.

Linton, Simi. *Claiming Disability: Knowledge and Identity*. New York and London: New York University Press, 1998.

Longmore, Paul K. "A Note on Language and the Social Identity of Disabled People." *American Behavioral Scientist* 28 (January/ February 1985): 419–23.

————. "Screening Stereotypes: Images of Disabled People in Television and Motion Pictures." In *Why I Burned My Book and Other Essays on Disability*, 131–46. Philadelphia, PA: Temple University Press, 2003.

Longmore, Paul K., and Lauri Umansky, eds. *The New Disability History: American Perspectives*. New York: New York University Press, 2001.

Lupton, Deborah. *Medicine as Culture: Illness, Disease and the Body in Western Societies*. London; Thousand Oaks: Sage, 1994.

Mace, Rodney. *Trafalgar Square: Emblem of Empire*. Southampton, UK: Camelot Press, 1976.

Mannix, Daniel P. *Freaks: We Who Are Not as Others*. New York: RE/Search Publications, 1999; 1969.

Mavor, Carol. "Obscenity in Art." In *Encyclopedia of Aesthetics,* vol. 1. Edited by Michael Kelly, 386–89. New York, Oxford: Oxford University Press, 1998.

McFarland, B., and T. Baker-Baumann. *Shame and Body Image: Culture and the Compulsive Eater*. Deerfield Beach, FL: Health Communications, 1990.

Merleau-Ponty, Maurice. *The Phenomenology of Perception*. Translated by Colin Smith. London: Routledge & Paul Kegan, 1962.

Miles, Malcolm. *Art, Space, and the City: Public Art and Urban Futures.* London and New York: Routledge, 1997.

Millett, Ann. "Disarming Venus: Disability and the Re-Vision of Art History," in *FemTAP: A Journal of Feminist Theory as Feminist Praxis* (Summer 2006).

———. "Exceeding the Frame: The Photography of Diane Arbus" in *Disability Studies Quarterly* 24, no. 4 (Fall 2004).

———. "Performing Amputation: The Photographs of Joel-Peter Witkin," in *Text and Performance Quarterly* 28 no. 1, 8 (January 2008), 8–42.

———. "Sculpting Body Ideals: *Alison Lapper Pregnant* and the Public Display of Disability," in *Disability Studies Quarterly* 28, no. 3 (Summer 2008).

———. "Sculpting Body Ideals: *Alison Lapper Pregnant* and the Public Display of Disability," in *Disability Studies Reader,* 3rd ed. (New York: Routledge, 2010).

Mitchell, David T., and Sharon L. Snyder. *The Body and Physical Difference: Discourses of Disability,* Ann Arbor: University of Michigan Press, 1997.

———. *Narrative Prosthesis: Disability and the Dependencies of Discourse.* Ann Arbor: University of Michigan Press, c. 2000.

———. *Vital Signs: Crip Culture Talks Back.* A Brace Yourselves Productions, 2001; 1996 (director's cut, 47 minutes).

Mitchell, Michael. *Monsters: Human Freaks in America's Gilded Age, the Photographs of Chas. Eisenmann.* Toronto, Canada: ECW Press, 2002.

Mulvey, Laura. *Visual and Other Pleasures.* Bloomington and Indianapolis: Indiana University Press, 1989.

Nathanson, Donald L. *Shame and Pride: Affect, Sex, and the Birth of the Self.* New York and London: W. W. Norton & Company, 1992.

Nead, Lynda. *The Female Nude: Art, Obscenity, and Sexuality.* London and New York: Routledge, 1992.

Nochlin, Linda. "The Imaginary Orient," from *The Politics of Vision: Essays on Nineteenth-Century Art and Society,* 33–59. New York: Harper & Row, c. 1989.

Norden, Martin F. *The Cinema of Isolation: A History of Physical Disability in the Movies.* New Brunswick, NJ: Rutgers University Press, c. 1994.

Olsen, Hanne. (Letter to the editor) "More than a message," *Guardian* (Saturday March 20, 2004).

Paré, Ambroise. *On Monsters and Marvels*. Translated by Janis L. Pallister. Chicago: University of Chicago Press, 1982; 1840.

Parry, Eugenia. *Joel-Peter Witkin*. London and New York: Phaidon, 2001.

Phelan, Peggy. *Unmarked: The Politics of Performance*. London: Routledge, 1993.

Pollock, Griselda. *Vision & Difference: Femininity, Feminism, and the Histories of Art*. London and New York: Routledge, 1988.

Preece, Robert. "Just a Load of Shock? An Interview with Marc Quinn." *Sculpture* 19, no. 8 (October 2000): 14–19.

Purcell, Rosamond. *Special Cases: Natural Anomalies and Historical Monsters*. San Francisco: Chronicle Books, c. 1997.

Rabelais, François. *The Portable Rabelais*. Translated and edited by Samuel Putnam. New York: Penguin Books, 1979; 1929.

Sayre, Henry M. *The Object of Performance: The American Avant-Garde since 1970*. Chicago and London: The University of Chicago Press, 1989.

Schneider, Rebecca. *The Explicit Body in Performance*. London and New York: Routledge, 1997.

Schnelle-Schneyder, Marlene. "Joel-Peter Witkin: Dream Work in Staged Pictures—The Demythologized World of Joel-Peter Witkin," *Camera Austria* 35 (1990): 30–36.

Schwenger, Peter. "Corpsing the Image," *Critical Inquiry* 26, no. 3 (Spring 2000): 395–413.

Searle, Adrian. "Arresting, strange and beautiful," *Guardian* (Friday September 16, 2005).

Seine, H. F., and S. Webster, eds. *Critical Issues in Public Art: Content, Context, and Controversy*. Washington and London: Smithsonian Institute Press, 1992.

Sekula, Allan. "The Body and the Archive." *October* 39 (Winter 1998): 3–64.

Selwood, Sara. *The Benefits of Public Art: The Polemics of Public Places*. Poole, UK: Policy Studies Institute Publications, 1995.

Shildrick, Margrit. *Embodying the Monster: Encounters with the Vulnerable Self*. London; Thousand Oaks, CA; New Delhi: Sage Publications, 2002.

Smith, Shawn Michelle. *American Archives: Gender, Race, and Class in Visual Culture.* Princeton, NJ: Princeton University Press, 1999.

———. *Photography on the Color Line: W. E. B. Du Bois, Race, and Visual Culture.* Durham: Duke University Press, 2004.

Snyder, Sharon L., Rosemarie Garland-Thomson, and Brenda Jo Brueggemann. *Disability Studies: Enabling the Humanities.* New York: Modern Language Association of America, 2002.

Sobieszek, Robert A. *Ghost in the Shell: Photography and the Human Soul, 1850–2000: Essays on Camera Portraiture.* Los Angeles: Los Angeles County Museum of Art; Cambridge, MA: MIT Press, c. 1999.

Solomon-Godeau, Abigail. *Photography at the Dock: Essays on Photographic History, Institutions, and Practices.* Minneapolis: University of Minnesota Press, c. 1991.

Sontag, Susan. *On Photography.* New York: Farrar, Straus, and Giroux, 1977.

Staff and agencies, "Livingstone unveils statue of 'modern heroine,'" *Guardian.* (Thursday September 15, 2005).

Stafford, Barbara Maria. *Body Criticism: Imaging the Unseen in Enlightenment Art and Medicine.* Cambridge, MA: MIT Press, 1991.

Stiker, Henri-Jacques. *A History of Disability.* Translated by William Sayers. Ann Arbor: University of Michigan Press, 1997.

Stoeckle, J. D., and G. A. White. *Plain Pictures of Plain Doctoring: Vernacular Expression in New Deal Medicine and Photography: 80 Photographs from the Farm Security Administration.* Cambridge, MA: MIT Press, c. 1985.

Tagg, John. *The Burden of Representation: Essays on Photographies and Histories.* Basingstoke, UK: Macmillan Education, 1988.

Terry, J., and J. Urla, eds. *Deviant Bodies Critical Perspectives on Difference in Science and Popular Culture.* Bloomington: Indiana University Press, 1995.

Turner, Bryan S. *The Body and Society: Explorations in Social Theory,* second edition. London: Thousand Oaks; New Delhi: Sage Publications, 1996.

———. *Regulating Bodies: Essays in Medical Sociology.* London; New York: Routledge, 1992.

Usherwood, Paul. "The Battle of Trafalgar Square." *Art Monthly* 2 no. 4 (March 2004): 43.

Villaseñor, Maria Christina. "The Witkin Carnival," *Performing Arts Journal* 18, no. 2 (May 1996): 77–82.

Warner, Marina. *Fantastic Metamorphoses, Other Worlds: Ways of Telling the Self.* New York: Oxford University Press, 2002.

———. *From the Beast to the Blonde.* New York: Farrar, Straus, and Giroux, 1995.

———. *Monuments and Maidens: The Allegory of the Female Form.* New York: Atheneum, 1985.

Wearing, Gillian. "The Eyes Have It," *Artforum* 42, no. 5 (February 2004): 125.

Weiss, Gail. *Body Images: Embodiment as Intercorporeality.* New York: Routledge, 1999.

Witkin, Joel-Peter. *Harms Way: Lust & Madness, Murder & Mayhem: A Book of Photographs.* Santa Fe, NM: Twin Palms Publishers, 1994.

———, ed. *Masterpieces of Medical Photography: Selections from the Burns Archive.* Captions by Stanley B. Burns. Pasadena, CA: Twelvetrees Press, 1987.

Wood, Brett. "Photo Mortis: Resurrecting Photographs of Crime and Death," *Art Papers* 24, no. 2 (March–April 2000): 18–23.

# Index

CPSIA information can be obtained at www.ICGtesting.com
Printed in the USA
BVOW011615111011

273347BV00003B/1/P